JANET MELROSE &
SHERYL NORMANDEAU

The Prairie Gardener's Go-To for

Small Spaces

T0160020

TOUCHWOOD

TouchWood Editions

touchwoodeditions.com

The information in this book is true and complete to the best of the authors' knowledge. All recommendations are made without guarantee on the part of the authors or the publisher.

Copy edited by Paula Marchese

Design and illustration by Tree Abraham

Photos by Janet Melrose and Sheryl Normandeau

CATALOGUING DATA AVAILABLE FROM LIBRARY AND ARCHIVES CANADA

ISBN 9781771513463 (print)

ISBN 9781771513470 (electronic)

TouchWood Editions acknowledges that the land on which we live and work is within the traditional territories of the Lkwungen (Esquimalt and Songhees), Malahat, Pacheedaht, Scia'new, T'Sou-ke and W̱SÁNEĆ (Pauquachin, Tsartlip, Tsawout, Tseycum) peoples.

We acknowledge the financial support of the Government of Canada through the Canada Book Fund, and the province of British Columbia through the Book Publishing Tax Credit.

This book was produced using FSC®-certified, acid-free papers, processed chlorine free, and printed with soya-based inks.

Printed in China

25 24 23 22 21   1 2 3 4 5

Dedicated to all prairie gardeners

Introduction 7

Introduction

Let us help you get inspired about growing in small spaces!

The ethos of small-space gardening is about much more than cramming all of the plants that you have into a smaller space. To garden successfully in a small space demands a little extra gardening know-how and some specialized techniques—it's not always as forgiving as when you have a big area to work with and can spread out. Every element must be in proportion to the space that you have, and your goal is to use every inch of it effectively and wisely. Sometimes it means you have to choose what to leave out, but this also means that you need to be very careful about what you keep. Our view is that successful small-space gardeners are a different breed, and what they create can be magical!

We're here to answer all of your big questions about small-space gardening and help boost your success! Whether you want to know about what types of growing media to use in containers or raised beds, how to properly fertilize and water your container plants, or how to get started in square foot gardening, we've got you covered! We're talking about the rewards of succession planting and catch cropping, and will give you valuable advice to help you build raised beds, wicking beds, and sub-irrigated planters. And, of course, we're supplying lists of prairie plants for every situation. We'll let you know which veggies and vines to grow vertically and what herbs and edible flowers are suitable for container growing, as well as small tree options for your postage stamp–sized yard and what plant selections can grow beneath these types of trees.

Learn how to make the most of *all* the gardening space you have!

—SHERYL NORMANDEAU & JANET MELROSE

Container Gardens

1

I want to buy some containers for my plants. Does the type of material they are made of matter?

Plastic is a popular and inexpensive material for containers.

There are so many kinds of containers out there, with more seemingly on the market every year!

Mankind has been using terracotta or earthenware since the paleolithic era, some 28,000 years ago. Terracotta is a baked clay used in art forms, building, and cooking—and, with the advent of agriculture, as containers for plants.

While gardeners are traditionalists when it comes to terracotta, we are also ready to adapt and adopt new materials for pots once we have a chance to try them out and to decide whether they work. The result is a huge range of planters to accommodate most gardeners' tastes, pocketbooks, and backs. Each choice has its own advantages as well as some drawbacks. Furthermore, selecting the right pots should also reflect the optimal environment for the plants that will be growing in them.

Clay pots have the benefit of being porous. Moisture and air can pass through the sides and are available to roots, which will grow out to the sides and be air-pruned. This encourages lateral branching and the development of a large healthy root ball. Excess moisture from heavy-handed watering can evaporate readily, though it is essential to purchase pots with existing drainage holes to avoid the potential for anaerobic conditions developing in waterlogged soils. Good-quality clay pots will have thick sides that moderate soil temperatures—a real bonus given the hugely variable temperature ranges on the prairies. Finally, the pots are heavy enough to not easily tip over. They also have that lovely earthy feel and look to them.

The weight of the pots can be a downside. Clay planters also need to be watered more frequently due to their porous nature. Made of baked earth, they are also relatively brittle, breaking more frequently than other choices. Choose high-quality clay pots over cheap ones. Because these pots, with their rolled rims and thicker sides, are formed and baked at higher temperatures, they are denser. Inexpensive clay pots have sharp sides and rims, as they are stamped by machine, rather than hand-formed. They may be made from inferior clay and baked at lower temperatures. They will chip or break readily.

Glazed terracotta planters are beautiful with interesting shapes and colours. The glaze is baked onto the outside of the planter at high temperatures, making them more durable and less permeable.

Plastic containers started appearing in the 1950s. They are inexpensive and easy to lift, due to their light weight. Shop wisely, as you'll find excellent-quality plastic pots as well as inferior ones. They are often made from recycled plastics, but the materials are inert and are considered safe for growing edibles. They come in a wide variety of sizes, shapes, and colours, and most are strong and durable. Plastic pots are not porous and retain water much longer, which is a real benefit in low humidity and windy conditions.

On the other hand, the lack of porosity can result in poor soil aeration. In plastic pots, roots are not air-pruned, and will continue to grow by circling the sides of the pot, with little lateral branching occurring. This can result in root-bound plants. Since there are fewer finer roots, the uptake of nutrients and water can be affected. Overwatering will lead to anaerobic conditions given the relative lack of evaporation. Plastic pots generally have thinner sides, and the material itself does not provide much in the way of insulation against variable temperatures. Overheating or near freezing of roots can occur.

Fibreglass and resin planters are widely available. They often resemble clay, stone, metal, and even wood in appearance, yet are reasonably lightweight and definitely durable. Fibreglass planters are made from a viscous polymer with fibreglass strands added, and are moulded rather than stamped. Resin planters are made from low-density polyethylene that is poured into moulds and baked. Both are strong, rigid, and ideal for many purposes. Not as inexpensive as plastic, but not as expensive as glazed ceramic or stone, they can absorb a lot of weather before starting to look the worse for wear. Being made of thicker material, they do offer some value for moderating soil temperatures but have the same disadvantages as plastic for curtailing root development.

Metal containers are also good options. The heavy cast-iron urns we are used to seeing are meant to be placed and stay in place, but there are lighter-weight sheet metal options available that are versatile and long-lasting. As with fibreglass and plastic, metal does not allow air to permeate the soil except through the surface and there is a real danger of overheating the soil if placed in full afternoon sun. I have a couple and keep them in a location where they get morning sun. Drill holes in the bottoms if they come without drainage holes.

In recent years fabric pots have made a splash! Geotextiles are made from synthetic polymers, either woven or not. Used originally in construction, agriculture, and ecosystem management for controlling erosion, and to improve and stabilize soils, fabric pots are sturdy, relatively long-lasting, and permeable to air and moisture. The modern version has been around since the 1950s but the practice of using cloth pots is old, going all the way back to the ancient Egyptians who would mix natural fibres into soil to hold it in place.

Most of the geotextiles used for gardening are non-woven, looking like thick black felt crafted into bags and containers of various shapes. There are many benefits to choosing a geotextile pot, as they are easily portable, and at the end of the season you just empty out the soil, shake them, fold them flat, and store. What I really like about them is that they encourage plant roots to grow out the sides and become air-pruned rather than becoming root-bound. The roots are happier

Geotextiles serve as durable and portable containers.

because air can enter into the soil, and excess water and heat can readily exit the soil mass as well during our warm summer days. The geotextile also serves to insulate the soil and roots when the weather turns colder.

There is always a fly in the ointment, and for geotextiles it is that you do need to water more often as the pots dry out faster. They also degrade over time and will need to be replaced. Made of synthetic materials, they are also not bio-degradable or recyclable. They are also very utilitarian and not usually considered aesthetically beautiful.

Make your choices based on what will be best for the health of your plants, with due consideration for your budget. Know the benefits and detriments for each and adjust your cultural practices to mitigate any disadvantages.[1] —JM

Terracotta pots have a timeless appeal that is favoured by gardeners.

Does the colour of a container affect how quickly a plant dries out, and how much heat it retains?

Yes, it does. If you've ever worn a black garment on a hot summer's day, you'll have an idea of how this works. Heat is easily absorbed by dark colours. If you pot your plants in black, dark green, or dark brown containers, the roots are going to warm up more (and more quickly) than if you put your plants in light-coloured containers. You may find you have to water more often. Furthermore, if things really heat up, the resulting stress on root systems can lead to a whole range of problems. The roots will not experience any significant growth during heat stress, which may lead to fewer blooms or less fruit. The plant may have trouble taking up water and nutrients. The leaves may discolour. Wilting and even death may occur. All that being said, there's no need to get rid of your dark-coloured pots. Unless you have situated them in an area fully exposed for long periods of time to blasting heat, you're probably not going to notice a massive difference for most plants. Any container plants situated in furnace-like conditions are more susceptible to heat stress, and it doesn't matter what colour the pots are. If you're concerned, use dark pots in dappled sunlight or part shade locations or indoors.[2] — SN

If I want to plant in a container that doesn't have drainage holes, what are my options?

Drainage is a must where plants are concerned—whether in-ground or in a container, but especially in a container, where the environment is restricted and the plant's roots are confined. If you can drill holes in the bottoms of your pots, that would solve the problem right away.

So—what if you can't put holes in the pot? Another option is to pot the plant in a so-called cache pot, a container with drainage. Insert the cache pot into your decorative, non-draining pot. (I do this with many of my houseplants as I like pretty containers that don't necessarily have holes in the bottoms.)

The last resort is to water extremely carefully—and I do mean *extremely*. If you don't have drainage in your pots, you could drown the roots easily and one round of overwatering is enough to do in your plants. If you have to do this, get the biggest container the plant will comfortably grow in (some plants don't like really big pots, so choose wisely). Truly, it's best to try to get a container with drainage and minimize the risk of doing possibly fatal damage.

Okay, I know you're asking: "But everyone says just to put gravel in the base of the pot!" Don't do this. When you think about how water percolates through the soil when you apply it, you'll understand why. As it trickles downward through the soil in the pot, some water is captured by the pores in the soil. The rest of it accumulates in a reservoir known as a water table. The soil is thoroughly saturated at the water table, but it isn't completely saturated above it. Healthy roots grow in the unsaturated zone and take up water from the saturated zone when they need it. If you put gravel in the bottom of the pot, you actually raise the level of water table and give your plant roots less room to grow. There is also an increased risk that the roots could end up sitting in water all of the time, and possibly rot.[3]—sn

What kind of soil mix should I put in containers?

The terminology around what to call the "soil" used in containers can be a minefield of confusion, along with a plethora of products all called something different to distinguish themselves.

"Soil" for containers is accurately described as growing medium or media, often as "soilless mixes." The common term "potting soil" usually contains no "soil," per se, though decades ago there usually was some garden soil in the mixes, and some mixes still do contain soil, which really adds to the confusion. We will never lose the term, so it is incumbent on us to understand what the differences are between all the products available.

Growing media for containers need to do three things: support the plants; encourage good root development; and allow air, water, and nutrients to get to the roots.

Before we get into what we should be using, let's discard the choices to avoid, such as topsoil, which is usually just another name for garden soil; planting soil; or even genuine potting soil. These are usually all dense mixes that contain sedge peat, as opposed to sphagnum peat moss. The texture is gritty or sandy and holds water in amounts detrimental to plant roots. It is often less expensive than other growing media. If in doubt, check the list of ingredients. If there isn't such a list, don't buy it. If it is too good to be true, it likely is.

The best growing medium for containers is a mix of sphagnum peat moss or coir fibre (ground coconut husks), perlite, and/or vermiculite, in varying proportions. Most contain compost. Other items, such as bark fines (ground-up bark and other forestry debris) and small amounts of lime that increase the pH of the mix to neutral, are often included. Wetting agents are sometimes added as dry peat moss or coir fibre is hydrophobic, initially repelling water. Made of polymers, they absorb water quickly, which means you can create a moist growing medium with less effort. I avoid growing media that contain wetting agents as they are not particularly biodegradable, and you are adding what is essentially plastic into your garden.

Good-quality growing medium is a key component in a showstopping container.

It is now common to find mixes containing mycorrhizal fungi (fungi found in garden soil). Mycorrhizal fungi promote good root structure through a symbiotic relationship with the plants.

I prefer not to use mixes that include additional fertilizer, often in slow-release formulations. If starting seeds, nutrients are not required as seeds in the initial stages of germination are using the food stored within the seeds. It is only once you have transplanted the seedlings that additional nutrients are needed for healthy growth.

My preference is to make my own growing medium. I aim for a light, loose, and porous mix, with good moisture retention. It should feel spongy when compressed in your hand. I also want it to have what I call "oomph," given our relative low humidity on the prairies, which dries out mixes more readily. I can change up its texture and nutrients to suit what I am growing.

For a container mix, I fill a wheelbarrow halfway with horticultural-grade sphagnum peat moss. I tend to avoid coir fibre because coconut trees grow in the tropics, and the product must be transported a huge distance to our gardens. The compressed blocks are hard to break up and hydrate. I also have a personal bias, from having been beaned by a—thankfully—young and small coconut, back when I was growing up in Trinidad. Coconuts can stay there!

To the peat I add a small bucket of good-quality perlite, a volcanic mineral that is heated until it looks like popcorn. Perlite aides in water retention and aeration, yet it does not alter the pH of the medium. Vermiculite, which is mica heated so that it resembles tiny sponges, is excellent at absorbing water. I find it can actually hold too much water, leading to waterlogged plants. A little goes a long way, if you do use it. Lately, pumice is becoming an option as it also performs the same function.

Next goes in two buckets or more of compost. I use either a good-quality bagged compost or sifted compost from my pile. The compost starts the process of developing healthy soil life in the containers along with some nutrients. I boost the mix with a trowelful of inert mycorrhizal fungi to promote root development.

Then I add a couple of trowels of fertilizer. This is usually fish meal and worm compost, plus kelp, feather, or alfalfa meal. After combining the mixture thoroughly, I water it so it is well moistened but not wet and get to work filling my containers.

There are many other recipes out there. Some have precise measurements, but I tend to go by feel. The end goal is that all-important "oomph" factor, where you just know that your plants are going to enjoy growing in it.[4] —JM

Some key ingredients in high-quality container growing media include sphagnum peat moss, compost, perlite, kelp meal, and mycorrhizal fungi.

Why shouldn't I use garden soil in containers?

Garden (or "field") soil, which is roughly composed of mineral particles (sand, silt, and clay), plus organic matter and hopefully 25 percent air pores and 25 percent water pores, is never suitable in containers since they have a small volume of growing medium and no interface with the ground they rest on. Garden soil can be very dense, especially the clay-based soils that dominate on the prairies. While your plants are cool with this in an in-ground setting, plopping them into a confined container filled with soil can be potentially life-threatening. The combination of a lack of oxygen and poor drainage becomes a huge issue. Cement-like soil can contribute to poor root development, as well as mould and rot. As an unwelcome bonus, you may also import weed seeds from your garden beds, and even some of the pests and soil-borne pathogens residing there. —SN & JM

Garden soil is too heavy to use in containers.

Should I change the growing medium in my containers every year?

The old adage that one's growing medium shouldn't be reused is taking a battering these days. Growing medium for containers is not cheap!

In days of yore—a.k.a. a few years ago—the materials for soilless mixes were relatively inexpensive, so I followed that maxim. At the end of each season, I would tip the mix out into my garden proper to help improve the texture of the clay-based soil I am constantly striving to lighten. Easier too than trying to find a place to store the stuff over winter.

The reasons for the practice of not reusing last year's mix are sound, ranging from the knowledge that peat or coir fibre degrades over time, becoming dust-like, to the certainty that any nutrients that were in the mix for last year's plants have been used. Potentially, weed seeds, insect eggs and larvae, and pathogens will have taken up residence by the end of the season. Not to mention that there are lots of roots, big and small, and likely leaves and whatnot in it.

Yet, there is that expense, and, if you do not have a handy garden to absorb it, then it is a waste we do not need to incur.

As I use a lot of growing medium, I now have a system that is similar to a four-year crop rotation schedule. I use my growing medium for different purposes each season, then by the autumn of the fourth year it goes into the garden. The first season, it gets used for high-value edibles, such as tomatoes or potatoes. The following season, I use it for other edibles, especially legumes and greens. The next season sees it being used in herb, strawberry, succulent, and perhaps mixed edible baskets. The last year, it serves for my annual flowers. Each year the plants being grown in it are less demanding overall, and not subject to the same pests. In this manner, I have some control over potential pathogens and insects being overwintered in the mix and it is less work to rejuvenate it in spring.

Each spring I take my tubs of overwintered medium, dump them out into my wheelbarrow, and sift for large pieces of roots and extraneous bits and pieces of other unwanted material. To restore the texture of the mix, I refresh it with lots

*Strawberries can be grown in reused,
disease-free growing medium.*

of compost, some perlite, and fertilizer, plus a small scoop of inert mycorrhizal fungi to promote excellent root growth.

Then it is ready for a new season!

A tip for storing used potting soil is to use stackable plastic tubs with lids. They are easy to label, and the covers keeps the mix dry over winter. Plus, the empty tubs stack together neatly out of the way during the growing season.[5]—JM

What are grow bags and how do I use them?

Grow bags are the rage!

Touted as a quick container option for those who don't want to or cannot invest in permanent containers, they are also versatile since they can be placed on balconies and other structures that cannot bear the weight of heavier containers. They are handy if you are in an area with contaminated soil or hard surfaces like parking lots. The best ones come with handles, so they can be readily toted or hefted.

Grow bags are versatile and low-cost. They are also permeable to air and moisture. Plants are happy growing in them as they are able to develop healthy root structures, with many lateral roots that have a greater ability to access nutrients, air, and water.

There are some downsides to using grow bags. It is necessary to water more often. Regularly checking soil moisture together with implementing water conservation strategies, such as mulching the topsoil, placing the bags in a tight grouping, not placing them in really windy locations, or providing a bit of a windbreak, will greatly aid in mitigating dry soil.

Grow bags are less durable than most pots and will need replacing more often. Some last only a season, others many years. They are rarely compostable, nor recyclable.

Grow bags come in a range of sizes from tiny to massive. They can be prefabricated, or made from DIY materials. They also come in a range of materials, from natural fibres, such as burlap, jute, hemp, and paper, to geotextiles and plastics. I have used the one cubic yard (0.76 cubic metre) bag that soil is delivered in very successfully as an instant raised bed. I filled it two feet (sixty centimetres) deep with growing medium and compost, and voila, it was good to go for the season. Burlap sacks are a good one-season option and have the added advantage of being free if you can get them from local coffee roasters. They are also biodegradable since by the end of the season the bottoms are usually rotted out. Likewise, the big paper bags for compostables make terrific low-cost, one use grow bags either on their own or placed side by side to make the size of the "bed" you want. Harvesting those potatoes is dead easy. Lift up the top of the bag and out fall the potatoes and growing medium! If you have a lot of reusable fabric bags in your closet, then they also can become grow bags, complete with handles. They won't last more than one season, but they can be a very funky container, indeed. I once made grow bags from pairs of old jeans. They worked like a dream! Anything goes, so long as the principles of grow bags are present.

Lately geotextiles have become grow bags, to the point that the words are almost interchangeable. A good-quality geotextile bag will have thick fabric with double-stitched seams. Ideally, it will have handles. I have had some of mine for five years and more, with the secret to their longevity being to really brush out all the soil and roots at the end of the season.

Potatoes and tomatoes are the most popular candidates for grow bags. Large plants like squash can also be successfully grown in such bags. Grow bags are also ideal for herbs and greens, though they will only need a bag about twelve inches (thirty centimetres) deep. Tall pole beans and peas work beautifully in grow bags with a trellis inserted into the bag at the time the seeds are sown. I have even used mine as full on flowerpots for annual edible flowers, with nasturtiums, borage, and calendula making for a bright and colourful pot.

Am I a fan of grow bags? You betcha![6] —JM

Those reusable fabric shopping bags that you have dozens of make excellent containers!

Can I grow potatoes in a bag or tub on my balcony?

Absolutely—and you have many options to do it in, including grow bags or fabric pots, potato towers, totes or bins, burlap sacks . . . your creativity is pretty much the limit. (Just don't use old tires—you don't want chemicals leaching into your food.) The containers must be deep for this to work properly. If your container is too shallow, you're not going to get many potatoes out of the deal. A full sun location is also a necessity for best results. Potatoes don't produce well in the shade.

If your container isn't made of fabric or doesn't have drainage holes, make sure you put some in at the base, so that the risk of root rot is minimized. Pour about four inches (ten centimetres) of a good container growing medium (either one you've made yourself or one you've bought premixed) into the base of the container. Plant seed potatoes five to seven inches (thirteen to eighteen centimetres) apart, then cover with approximately three inches (eight centimetres) of the medium. Place the container in your sunny location and keep up with a regular watering schedule. Do not overwater at any time. Every two weeks throughout the growing season, add a dilution of liquid organic fertilizer, either balanced 20-20-20 or, even better, 10-20-20.

Once the potatoes begin to grow and have reached about three inches (eight centimetres) in height, then you need to add more growing medium. Go ahead and bury some of the lower foliage. Maintain regular applications of water. If your plants get super large, you may have to add medium again. Harvest when the plants are ready. (You can, of course, reach in and sneak out baby potatoes a little early, when needed for the barbecue grill!) Remember, not all potatoes flower, so that's not the most reliable way to judge when to harvest. If you're looking for full-sized potatoes, wait to grab them about two to three weeks after the plant's foliage has died back.[7] —SN & JM

What are global buckets and sub-irrigated planters and how can I make them?

Sub-irrigated planters are created from inexpensive, readily available materials. Note the pipe on each planter; it is used to carry water down into the reservoir

Sub-irrigated planters (SIPs) are just as the name suggests—they are containers that have a reservoir beneath the growing medium. The water is easy for plants to take up whenever required and is just as simple for gardeners to top off. Global buckets are one type of SIP using food-grade approved five-gallon (nineteen-litre) pails.

Global buckets were created by two American high school students, Max and Grant Buster, as a means to cheaply grow food in drought-stricken continents such as Africa. They are so easy to make and use that they are now widely used pretty much anywhere there is enough sunlight. There are two buckets in the system: the lower one is a reservoir for water, while the upper one holds the growing medium and plant. The upper bucket has a hole in the base where a container with slit sides is placed. This container is filled with soil and it sits in the water, allowing for water to be wicked up through the system. Another hole is cut into the base of the upper bucket to allow for insertion of a pipe down into the reservoir. When the reservoir is low, the gardener can simply pour water into the pipe. (If you have multiple buckets to water, you can use siphon hoses and allow atmospheric pressure to do the work for you.)

A common type of SIP is made from five-gallon (nineteen-litre) food-grade pails.

To plant your global bucket, sprinkle some slow-release fertilizer on top of the growing medium and cover the whole top of the bucket with part of a black plastic garbage bag, leaving the pipe sticking up. You won't be opening up the bag while the plant is alive—the system has enough nutrients to feed the plant, and you are taking care of the water. By covering the growing medium, water is less likely to evaporate, and you don't have to weed. Slice open an X shape in the middle of the bag and carefully pot up your plant. (Tomatoes work super well in global buckets, but most veggies are suitable.) Note that you also have the option of not covering the SIP with a plastic bag—you can leave the top open and add a mulch, such as straw, instead. The mulch will help conserve moisture and prevent weeds.

Gardeners are constantly working with materials they may have on hand, and they tend to be a creative lot, so if you browse the internet, you'll see countless ways to make other types of SIPs. One famous type—the one that inspired the Buster boys—is a rectangular box on casters. (Portability is a big part of the appeal of these types of planters.) Instead of a second box being placed inside the first one, it uses a screen to cover the reservoir at the base of the box. In this way, the soil sits on top of the reservoir, and water is wicked upwards. A tube is used to bring water to the reservoir. Growing medium and fertilizer are added, and then the whole thing is covered with a cloth. The gardener cuts slits into the cloth to plant—and voila! Instant SIP. These sorts of containers are fabulous for use in small spaces, and you don't need to babysit them constantly to add inputs of water and fertilizer.

Depending on what you're using for materials, SIPs can be a bit of an eyesore, and if you're using the bucket style, you may be growing only one plant per bucket, which means you'll need several buckets to grow a lot of food. But with the use of free or inexpensive materials and the minimal labour required, you may decide this is worth a try![5]—SN

Can I keep my empty containers outside over winter?

If at all possible, I recommend bringing containers into an area where they cannot freeze. Terracotta and ceramic pots may crack and break if they have even the tiniest chips or fractures and are subjected to cycles of freezing and thawing. Resin and plastic containers will occasionally do the same. I'll never forget the spring I went over to a friend's house to help plant a bunch of containers for her front yard. The previous autumn, she had purchased several beautiful clay pots from a garden centre and then stacked them beneath a tarp behind her garage. Guess what we uncovered? A pile of pretty painted clay shards. She had purchased the pots at a discount, which lessened the hurt somewhat, but it was still upsetting.

If you have the space to keep your pots separated, it's best to do that instead of stacking them. Store them upside down so that moisture, dead insects, and other interesting things don't accumulate. — SN

Terracotta pots are prone to breakage if they are not stored properly over the winter.

How do I clean and sanitize my containers before planting?

There is a great temptation come spring to skip an essential step in good garden hygiene practices and simply fill last year's planters with your soil mix and get gardening.

Our containers are going to get dirty anyway, so why clean them beforehand?

Last year's planters may have deposits of salts and minerals, often seen as white coating on the sides or rims of pots, which, if left, may cause problems with nutrient uptake and potential burning of stems and roots when in contact with the salts. Additionally, there may be disease-causing pathogens in leftover soil or clinging to the sides of the pots, and occasionally eggs of our favourite bugs.

To clean portable planters, use a stiff brush to remove the remaining soil. A word to the wise: do a good job of this before dunking the containers into the sink. Soil going down the drain can lead to a pricey plumbing bill.

Inspect the planters (especially unglazed ones) for damage. If salts and minerals are really stuck on, use a blunt knife to scrape them away. Then immerse the pots in a tub with soapy water and give them a good scrubbing. Follow up with a soak in warm water with the addition of a cup of pickling vinegar, horticultural vinegar, or hydrogen peroxide.

Many people will recommend a 10 percent bleach solution for the rinse, but I stopped doing so once I found out that bleach combined with organic compounds can form organochlorines. These are known carcinogens and neurotoxins.

Large containers, where the growing medium remains inside from year to year, should at least be inspected and any salts on the edges and sides removed. It is a good idea to remove one-third of the growing medium to rejuvenate the mix with extra compost and nutrients. That will also remove salts in the mix as well as overwintering insects.

Should winter hold off, this is one job I like to do as the season closes down as it give me a lot of satisfaction to see my planters clean. Then they are ready for the spring planting rush![9] —JM

Containers need a little TLC *before you put them into storage for the winter.*

I have a large planter box or container to fill. Can I line the bottom with something so that I don't have to spend so much money on soil?

Large containers can be difficult to move when filled, and putting that much growing medium in them can be expensive. Placing inert materials that won't absorb moisture nor break down readily in the bottom of the container can make a real difference, both in cost and in a possible back sprain when it needs to be shifted.

A word of caution: do not create a top-heavy container that can fall over easily, possibly causing injury to someone. Place heavy stones in the bottoms of such planters to provide a counterweight and make the planters stable before going further.

Drainage is another consideration. Ensure you are using a planter with a generous, unclogged drainage hole. The fill is not meant to enhance drainage; it is in place to lighten the weight and decrease the amount of growing medium required.

Good candidates for fill include durable plastics that will not crush under the weight of the soil above. My favourites are the pots that our new shrubs and perennials come in. I place them upside down in the container in an even layer, and don't worry if there are spaces between them.

I never use foam or Styrofoam of any sort, including the packing peanuts. The lightweight material will compact over time and plant roots can grow into it. Worst of all: when you take the soil out of the container at some point to refresh it, the foam breaks up easily.

Another method is to use decaying organic material such as small branches, twigs, and leaves, which will contribute to establishing healthy soil life within the container. The materials do break down over time but it is a good trade-off for the benefits.

Some gardeners put mesh across the fill to deter soil from sifting down into the fill. I prefer to let the soil do that, so that there isn't a distinct layer between the soil above and the fill below. There is less chance of an oversaturated water table developing.[10] —JM

What are the best watering practices for container gardens and raised beds?

Watering your garden should be a deliberate act, not a passing task to be done in a hurry and haphazardly. It should be done with thought and care. You need to take the time to test to see if the bed or containers need to be watered, to watch the water percolate into the soil or growing medium, and to inspect what is growing and how well.

I love watering, just like I love to weed, because it brings me into a deliberate act of observing the garden and all that is going on in it. I consider ironing a chore, so I don't iron and wear wrinkled clothes. But if we view watering as a chore, we don't get wrinkled plants. We get wilted and dead ones. So, the best watering practice of all is to be in the right mindset!

Get into the habit of checking to see if watering is needed. A brief rain shower can fool us into thinking that the soil is wet enough; but, by the same token, a good rain could make the soil wet all through the soil profile. To test, insert your fingers into the soil at least three inches (eight centimetres) toward the location of the roots. It can be misleading to consider the wilting of foliage as an indicator that a plant needs water, as wilting can also be a symptom of overwatering. Then, too, many plants will wilt naturally in the hot sun. They gently sag until the worst of the heat is over, then, like magic, they straighten up again.

When watering, watch how fast it disappears. For raised beds I have a ten-second rule. If the water is absorbed into the ground in less than ten seconds, I water again and watch, until I see the water sitting on the surface for that long before slowly sinking in. Containers are a little trickier, because there is less growing medium, so my rule is to water till it runs out of the bottom of the container. Then I come back in a bit and do it again. This gives the plant roots time to start taking up the water, and then they get a bit more to hold them over until next time.

Watering is best done in the early morning, when the day is cooler, allowing the moisture to get right into the soil and into the roots before the heat of the day works to evaporate moisture from the soil. The next best time is the early evening,

Mulch is a valuable addition to the garden, helping to conserve soil moisture.

so that any water on the foliage can dry before the night turns cool. If you can't do either of those, water when you are able to do so; it's better than not at all.

Water at the soil level, not from above. This ensures that the water gets where it needs to be, especially when plants are mature, and the leaf canopy is dense. Mulching keeps more moisture in the soil longer and moderates soil temperatures and thus evaporation rates.

While it is good to establish a regular schedule for watering so we get in the habit, always be flexible and water more often on days when it is hot or windy. Containers, in particular, will dry out faster in those conditions. We may still need to check the soil on cooler days and if there is just a little rain. If we have a rigid schedule, we can end up drowning our plants or letting them die of thirst.

Although not always practical, hand-watering is best as you are in close proximity to the plants and you can really pay attention to them. A watering wand allows you to direct the flow of water and control the rate of application, so you don't

An olla is a useful, inexpensive passive watering device.

flood the plants all at once. The worst habit to get into is to direct a stream of water from afar and hope that it gets to where it should!

There are lots of passive watering devices on the market and DIY versions too. My number one favourite device is an ancient one called an olla, pronounced *"oya."* After a clay pot is sunk into the soil or growing medium, it is then filled with water and will release its moisture through the pores of the clay as the soil draws it out. It is an effective way to keep the soil moist where it counts and will reduce your watering bill. It is not as practical for containers, but there are skinny versions you can make yourself from pop bottles punctured on the sides and inserted into the soil to allow the water to enter the soil through an underground drip system. There are also many drip irrigation systems on the market. But do not rely on watering devices to do the job without your supervision. It is through your careful observation and testing that you can ensure the soil is being kept constantly moist, but not too wet, and that the plants you are caring for are happy and healthy.

PS. I usually water with a cup of coffee or other moisture intake device in my hand so I get watered, too![11] —JM

Should I use hydrogel/moisture-retaining crystals for my container plants?

Hydrogel, water beads, moisture beads, and soil moisture crystals are all names for man-made synthesized water-absorbing polymers. They are cross-linked poly-acrylamide polymers (PAM), made up of water-insoluble acrylamide and potassium acrylate.[12] Water is absorbed through osmosis, and the white powder-like crystals absorb anywhere between 300 and 500 times their weight in water and become gel-like, releasing stored moisture as the surrounding medium dries, and then will reabsorb moisture when it is introduced. The crystals are biodegradable, lasting anywhere from two to seven years before completely breaking down. They are sold as powders or variously sized beads.

I have always been a bit dubious of them, especially since I am a rather frugal gardener and avoid anything that boosts the price of something without definite proof that it is worth the cost. So, I took them for a test drive, adding the correct volume to the soil for a plant, and planted another, similar plant in my regular potting soil. Yes, the polymers took up a ton of water initially, and, no, I didn't have to water the one with the polymer in it as frequently. Both plants seemed to grow about the same. But I still had to check each plant as frequently, determine whether they needed water or not, and monitor their health. Part of the joy in gardening is the actual tending and caring for plants. My conclusion was that they might be useful for my hanging baskets that dry out faster, but otherwise, I could take them or leave them.

Hydrogel polymers are also being touted for regular garden soil, especially in areas where drought is an issue. To my mind, there is no substitute for taking the time to build up soil with organic matter, which absorbs and retains significant amounts of moisture, and provides nutrients to soil life and plants. Their effectiveness in garden soil is also dependent on a variety of factors, including the makeup of one's mineral soil, the presence of fertilizers and amendments, and the vast chemical interactions between them all.

What really got my attention, however, was the fact that although they are considered biodegradable, the polymers break down into their component molecules and remain in the environment. Additionally, acrylamide is known to be a neurotoxin for human beings and is possibly carcinogenic.

That did it for me. I dumped the soil with the hydrogels into a bag and into the garbage. I'll water my hanging baskets and containers as I always do, with care and attention, and treat my plants to the best compost-amended, moisture-retentive, and nutrient-rich medium I can.[13] —JM

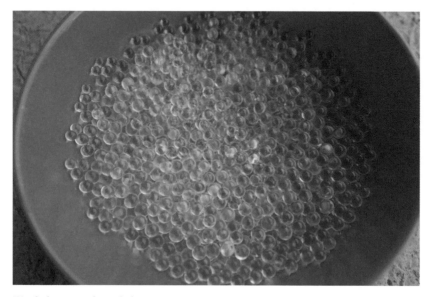

Weigh the pros and cons before deciding to use hydrogel polymers.

I have read that you can put disposable diapers in your containers to keep the soil from drying out. Should I do this?

Okay, let's be clear—according to proponents of this idea, you're not putting the *whole* diaper in the pot; you're just cutting it open, removing the absorbent crystals (hydrogels) inside, and then placing those into the planter. The rest of the diaper then goes into the landfill—yuck! If you *really* feel you need to use hydrogels (and we're not recommending that you do so), just purchase a container of some rated for actual horticultural use, and save the diapers for the little ones.—SN

How often should I fertilize my container plants throughout the growing season?

If your growing medium contains a slow-release fertilizer or if you choose to use a slow-release fertilizer at planting time, then you should be good to go without fertilizer for approximately two months. If the edible plants you are growing are heavy feeders, you can add a balanced water-soluble fertilizer such as 20-20-20 after a month and top up every month thereafter.

If you're not using a slow-release fertilizer and you're growing flowering plants, you can use a water-soluble fertilizer specifically formulated for blooms. Edibles should receive a broader range of minerals and nutrients for them to taste great. Either use an organic liquid fertilizer formulated for edibles or augment the growing medium with sprinkles of worm compost or other granular fertilizers and tickle them into the medium to get them working for your plants. — SN & JM

Keep your container plants going well into autumn with regular additions of nutrients over the growing season.

I'm seeing what looks like salt building up on top of the soil in my containers. What is happening, and how can I prevent it?

Salts are naturally found in our water, and in all garden soil, soilless mixes, and fertilizers. As plants uptake water and nutrients, or as the planting medium dries out through surface evaporation, salts remain. They can be visible as tan crusts on the sides of containers or even on top of the soil mix. White deposits can often be seen on the outside of unglazed clay pots.

In-ground beds can usually avoid the buildup as salts are naturally leached through the soil profile and enter the subsoil. They eventually reach the ground-water and are drained away.

However, salt buildup in planters is almost the norm. When the buildup of salt in planters becomes visible, the concentrations are likely preventing plants from

Flushing excess salts from containers can promote better health for your plants. This bay laurel is showing signs of new growth after such a treatment.

Salts from irrigation water and fertilizers may be deposited on unglazed clay containers.

uptaking nutrients and possibly water. Root damage may occur. In excessive amounts, salts can literally pull water out of plant roots and cause plant death.

Signs of a high salt concentration in plants may include tipburn and dieback of leaves; aborting of new growth at the growth points; and little to no growth and wilting, even when soil moisture is good.

Preventing salt buildup is a multipronged approach. First, avoid using synthetic fertilizers, which are typically mineral salts in a form that is readily taken up by plants. When these fertilizers are used, any excess not absorbed by plants stays in the soil as crystals. Overfertilizing with these types of fertilizers accelerates salt accumulation.

Second, make sure that your planter has good drainage and that the medium being used is moisture retentive but well-draining.

Third, avoid using tap water as much as possible. It contains chlorine and other chemicals as well as dissolved solids. Rainwater and snowmelt are the best options, but a good second choice is potable water that has been allowed to stand for twenty-four hours to allow off-gassing of some of the chemicals. When watering, use enough water to go through the soil profile and drain out of the bottom. Avoid leaving plants in standing water because the salts can be reabsorbed into the soil.

Finally, maintain a consistent fertilization schedule and follow directions for diluting fertilizers. They are usually highly concentrated, and we gardeners tend to use a heavy hand. More is not better in this instance!

A long-term prevention plan, especially for plants growing year-round, is to perform a flush on a regular basis. If you observe signs and symptoms of a high salt level, the remedy is to flush the salt out with water roughly two to three times the volume of soil and allow excess water to drain out. You may need to do a number of flushes to remove all the salts. Leave the planter alone for a few days and see if the plants perk up and resume growing. At that point, you can start fertilizing again with a re-established schedule.

If the planter is a well-established one with a serious salt problem, I have resorted to completely taking the plant out of the pot and washing its roots, stems, and foliage in tepid water to remove all the salts around the plant parts. Then I repot it in fresh potting soil. A bay laurel I had for years hadn't grown for a good six months, and within a few days after this treatment, I had new leaves growing![14]—JM

What are some good tips for potting up a showstopping flower container/hanging basket?

Everything has been carefully considered in this appealing arrangement, from the container to the plant selections and colours.

Great-looking hanging baskets don't happen by chance but rather by design! Once you get the hang of it, they are easy to make and maintain. Plus, you get the fun of creating something that will not look like all the others on the block!

Before you start, consider where your basket will hang: Will it be in lots of sun or part shade? Out of the prevailing winds or totally exposed? Under the rain shadow of eaves or under the branches of dense trees? The conditions the basket will face over the season may dictate the type of basket or container that you use, as well as the watering regime. Bigger, deeper containers with plants that tolerate drought-like conditions are best for hot, sunny, and windy exposures. In a calm, shady spot, use moss or coir fibre planters where plants that enjoy moist, shady conditions can be tucked through the sides of the container as well as on top.

When choosing containers, go for ones that are deeper and larger than you *think* you might need. Plants in hanging baskets are grouped more densely than normal, in small amounts of growing medium. A more spacious container will give them the opportunity to develop better root systems. Aim for lots of aeration, plus good moisture retention around the roots. I avoid plastic pots as they get really hot in the sun. Plants are more likely to become root-bound and damaged. My preference is for wire baskets that I can line with coir fibre, even though it means I will need to irrigate them more often. For a casual aesthetic, I even use thick burlap sacks cut to fit the basket.

The growing medium you choose should be top quality, sphagnum peat moss or coir fibre with perlite. I add extra compost, so it doesn't dry out as easily.

Establish a regular fertilizer regime to promote flowering and overall plant growth. I prefer to fertilize every time I water using a diluted solution rather than once or twice a month, as I always forget when it was that I last fertilized. When watering, water slowly and until the water is dripping out of the bottom of the container or basket. I will go back and add a second dose of water to confirm that the growing medium has had time to absorb all the water. I may even do a third pass to make sure. Hanging baskets are thirsty all the time, so keep up with the watering!

When choosing your plants, resist the urge to plant larger ones already in flower. Go for the smaller plants, so that they can concentrate on establishing their roots before blooming. As well, do not overplant a basket. We want our baskets to be dense, but we also need to respect the size each plant will achieve over time, or they will all suffer from overcrowding. Start early in the season, when there is a good selection of plants in the garden centres, and then let your selections grow in the first month before hanging them up. I like to finish off a basket and help conserve moisture by mulching with moss once the plants are nicely established.

Have fun![15] —JM

Creative and whimsical,
these kitchen colanders are
enjoying a new life housing
strawberries.

These begonias pop with colour in a hanging basket designed for a spot in part shade.

How do I deadhead flowers?

"Deadheading" is a very descriptive—if not slightly macabre—term: it involves snipping off the flowers of plants after they are finished blooming. Deadheading is an important step in maintaining the beauty and tidiness of plants. To do the task, use a pair of sharp, long-bladed scissors or a pair of hand pruners. Make sure your cuts are clean and just below the flowers. If the stems are soft, not woody, you may be able to just pinch off individual flowers with your fingertips.

If you love blue flax and catmint, you'll know that to say they reseed freely is a huge understatement. For plants like these, deadheading the flowers immediately after they are spent will save you the trouble of pulling up all those volunteers later (unless, of course, you want them!). If there are lots of faded blooms, you can just give the plant a haircut and mow many off at once. Don't trim back more than one-third of the plant.

Bear in mind that, much like weeding, deadheading is a job that must be done repeatedly. You can't just deadhead and forget about it. If you want to save seeds, then you can skip the task altogether. —SN

How can I keep my hanging baskets looking lush and full of blooms all summer?

Hanging baskets are prone to looking rather bedraggled by midsummer. Simply put, we place those plants under a lot of stress by siting them way up high in limited growing medium instead of where they are meant to be, in the ground with access to lots of space, nutrients, and water.

To reduce the stressors and prolong blooming time, continue to water thoroughly and fertilize on a regular schedule. For additional TLC, top-dress the basket with a generous handful of worm compost for slow-release nutrients.

A mid-season pick-me-up can really help. Take down the basket and inspect the plants. Look for those that are on their last legs, and check whether the growing medium has diminished. Monitor for pests. If the plants are too crowded, consider removing a couple to give space to the rest. Rather than digging them out, simply snip the stems off at the base.

Give the plants a judicious haircut, especially those that have grown leggy, making sure to snip stems just above where the next set of leaves are to promote branching. Deadhead spent blooms for tidiness. Add another handful or so of worm compost to fill up the baskets' growing medium and offer a good watering. The basket should really take off again and reward you with a great show for the rest of the season.[16] —JM

Can I bring my houseplants outdoors for the summer?

Yes, absolutely—with a few important considerations.

Exposure to everything Mother Nature has to throw at them can be a huge problem for pampered houseplants. Think about what you would do if you had never left your house in your life and were suddenly plopped out into a combination of scorching sun, drying winds, cold, rain, and hail. (And as we know on the prairies, sometimes all of these can happen in a single twenty-four-hour period.) And on top of all of that, there are insects such as fungus gnats to contend with.

That's not to say you shouldn't create a beautiful tropical oasis with your houseplants on your patio or deck. Just mitigate some of the potential problems. Prepare your houseplants for life outdoors by acclimatizing them to their new environment. Although you're not going to put your houseplants outside until it is warm enough to do so, they'll still need to adjust to the temperature and the humidity levels. Take them outside and place them in a sheltered spot out of direct sunlight and wind for just a few hours a day for a week or two before you commit to leaving them outside overnight. (And if the overnight temperatures tend to plummet in your region, even at the height of summer, maybe rethink leaving them out when the sun goes down.)

When selecting an outdoor site for your houseplants, it is ideal if you can give them a roof over their heads, so that they aren't drowned by large rainstorms or exposed to hailstones. Keep them out of blasting, drying winds. Ensure you have matched their sunlight requirements to your location—don't put a sun lover in deep shade or vice versa. Maintain a regular watering and fertilizing schedule that suits the plant's individual needs, and don't forget to monitor for signs of pests and diseases.

When summer begins to wane, you'll need to perform another period of acclimatization—this time, getting your houseplants ready for life back inside the house. Bring them in for a few hours each day for a couple of weeks. (Don't forget to treat them for fungus gnats or you'll regret it later!) Do not wait too long to bring your houseplants indoors in the fall or you could risk losing them all to frost. —SN

Houseplants such as Boston fern and inch plant will easily adapt to their summer home.

Can I bring herbs and other annual plants indoors for winter? How should I prepare them for the transition?

Absolutely! Some gardeners prefer to just have their tender herbs hibernate for the winter in a cool dark room and replant them outside when the growing season returns. Others bring them inside to keep them growing for fresh herbs throughout the winter.

Annual herbs are impossible to bring indoors. They have completed their life cycle by setting seed in late summer and are meant to die, no matter how much we would prefer otherwise. Instead, collect their seeds and start new plants inside for use over the winter. Chervil, cilantro, borage, and dill are all rewarding and easy to start inside. I also include basil in this category, although it is a perennial, as we prefer to use the tender and mild-tasting leaves of newly grown seedlings rather than the tougher, stronger-tasting ones from a mature plant. Likewise, annual flowering plants are never worth the effort. Our homes just do not have the right conditions for them to continue flowering for long. Much as it pains us, at the end of the season we need to let them die a dignified death.

Biennials are possible to bring inside, but I don't often do so, except perhaps a really healthy parsley plant. They are supposed to die back to the crown in the fall, and in the case of parsley, they have long taproots, so it isn't worth the effort to dig them up only to see them dwindle over the next couple of months. Instead I sometimes attempt to overwinter a few outside in the hope that they return in spring, and I can gather their seeds.

Hardy perennial herbs such as tarragon, sorrel, chives, hyssop, chamomile, thyme, oregano, and some mints may be left outside, after a good harvest, to brave the winter. There is a temptation to bring them all in, but space is always a consideration. Plus, I have found over the years that sage, thyme, and oregano only barely survive indoors, with their flavours becoming stronger and almost unpleasant. Best to leave them well mulched and outside to see if they will survive whatever winter throws at them. If any are growing in containers, transplant them into a garden bed since they won't overwinter in a container.

Tender perennials are another matter—especially those unusual or expensive herbs you have nurtured all season long—as are tender foliage or flowering perennials such as zonal geraniums, ivy, and lily of the Nile (*Agapanthus africanus*). It's definitely worth the effort to move them inside.

To prepare your plants for overwintering indoors, start early, before the night temperatures drop. Make your plant selections and inspect them to ensure that they are disease-free. Remove them from their containers or beds and shake off as much of the soil as you are able to, without damaging the roots.

Because I have brought in many insects and other "friends" over the years—including, on one memorable occasion, slugs of all things—I take several preventive steps. Once I have released most of the soil from the plant, I dunk the whole thing—roots, stem, leaves, and all—in a tub of lukewarm water. I let it soak until the rest of the soil loosens from the roots, then I remove the plant, tip out the water, and refill the tub for another quick soak, repeating again, if needed. I am thorough: the goal is to flush away any insect adults, larvae, or eggs from the root ball and leaves. Then I repot the plant in some fresh soilless mix, making sure to spread the roots out nicely, give it a nice drink (I have one, too!), and allow it to settle in. If it remains nice outside, I put the plants out during the day, but enclosed in floating row cover to keep any opportunistic bugs away. When I've taken a look at the weather forecast, and it looks like the plants will need to come indoors, they're ready. It is amazing how well the plants respond to this treatment, often with new growth occurring in days.

As most of us want to continue harvesting our herbs, they need to be overwintered under grow lights. Window ledges at our latitudes during the winter months

Best herbs to overwinter

* Bay laurel
* Rosemary
* Ginger
* Lemon grass
* Lemon verbena

* Myrtle
* Garlic chives
* Spanish lavender
* Winter savory—**JM**

These geraniums (Pelargonium spp.) are enjoying a luxurious winter vacation indoors in a sunny window.

simply do not get the necessary light and energy from the sun. Do not overwater, as many of these herb plants will quickly go south if their soil is waterlogged. If low humidity is an issue, place them in saucers filled with pebbles and water, but be careful to not let the plants sit in the water. The water will evaporate and moderate the humidity around the plants.

Keep a small fan handy for air circulation. As well, monitor for "friends" at all times. I usually do not fertilize until March since I include worm compost in my soilless mix, which gives my plants enough nutrients for the first few months.

Then enjoy them. There is profound satisfaction to be had from overwintering these plants![17] —JM

Can I overwinter perennial flowers, trees, and shrubs in containers outdoors?

Let's just say there are no guarantees that you will have success. But you can certainly try! Here are a few options to consider:

Get your plants in-ground before it freezes, pot and all. Bury the container to the rim and water after planting. Mulch with some dried leaves around the base of the plant, but do not cover it.

If you're overwintering trees and shrubs, you can forgo the containers and pop them directly into the ground for the winter. Be sure to mulch them with dried leaves or bark mulch. Borderline tender plants, such as some roses and hydrangeas, can be set into trenches dug in the soil and covered with leaves, straw, compost, or burlap.

You can try placing the containers into a garage that is cool but kept just above freezing temperatures in the winter. Too much warmth will break the dormancy of the plants and possibly damage them.

Occasionally, a plant will survive if you keep the container outside through the winter. It helps if the container is large and holds a lot of soil, which acts as an insulator. Some gardeners also swear that plants that overwinter outside must be hardy to at least two zones colder than what your climate is rated for. That means if your region is zone four, to make it through the winter, your trees or shrubs must have a hardiness zone of two. It's not a hard and fast rule, and, like I said, you'll be fortunate if the plant survives. A gardener I knew years ago would try to insulate his containers further by wrapping them in bubble wrap or Styrofoam, and it looked ridiculous, but he did manage to save a few. Not all of them, however. Bear in mind, I live in an area where the winters are plagued with constant freeze and thaw cycles, and that doesn't help matters.

One more point to make if you decide to try this: woody plants tend to be a bit more cold hardy than soft-stemmed ones, so your trees and shrubs may have a better chance than some of your herbaceous perennials.[18] —SN

Can I plant spring-flowering geophytes (bulbs) such as tulips in containers and have them overwinter and bloom?

Planting bulbs in containers that are going to be outside on the prairies during the winter with no added protection is a sure way to kill off your bulbs. Planted in-ground, surrounded by soil, other plant roots, snow cover, and mulch, they do fine, with only half-hardy ones like hyacinths not really being happy with the wintry conditions. In containers the cold comes in from all sides, and the freezing/thawing action when we have milder weather spells doom for any and all spring-flowering bulbs, except for those in huge containers.

Yet we all enjoy pots of bulbs in containers come spring.

One way to accomplish this is to plant a container just as you want it to be come spring, then sink it, pot and all, in a handy space in the garden and top it with mulch. To get it out easily without waiting for everything to thaw, line the hole with straw and have a cradle of rope or a burlap sack enclosing the pot as something to grasp onto when getting it out. Another method is to plant the container, make sure it is moist but not wet, and keep it in an unheated garage well in the back, away from the doors and against the wall of the house. A handy cold cellar works, too.

If you are wanting a lot of containers with bulbs, you can also try potting them, then grouping them together and tarping them securely in a cold area of the garden, away from the sun and warm winds, and insulating the whole mass with straw and dried leaves. I had some success with this strategy one year as an experiment, and lost only a couple of pots. I was lucky though as it was a milder than normal winter with few chinooks.

A word to the wise: be sure to use pots that are not prone to cracking as the medium, plus moisture, will make them especially vulnerable.[19] —JM

How do I deal with fungus gnats?

Fungus gnats (part of the Sciaridae family) are the bane of many a gardener. I don't think I've met a gardener who hasn't had to battle them at some point or another.

You know that you have fungus gnats, as opposed to fruit flies, if you see them crawling around the edges of pots or on soil. Fungus gnats also love to fly around just in front of you, as they are attracted to the CO_2 that we exhale. They tend to stay close to plants and not migrate to where fruit, compost, or garbage may be. Fruit flies, on the other hand, go for fruit and rotting food. Yuck!

Fungus gnats arrive at your home in contaminated potting soil, from the outdoors, or alongside plants that you have purchased. (The gnats may have originated in the greenhouse where the plants were raised.) In other words, from just about anywhere. They are small, maybe ⅛ inch (3 millimetres) long. They have black heads and look like tiny mosquitoes. Unlike mosquitoes, they are harmless to humans and are not known to carry any pathogens that affect us. They can damage plant roots, and they potentially carry the fungus that causes "damping off," a major killer of small seedlings. On the other hand, they have a necessary role in consuming organic matter and converting the nutrients to forms that plants can use. We just want them to do it outside!

To control fungus gnats, you need to know their life cycle. Each adult lives only about a week, but before a female dies, she lays hundreds of eggs in the top layer of the medium in our pots. After the eggs hatch, they remain in the larval stage for about two weeks, consuming soil debris and fungi. Adults barely eat, mostly sipping nectar or water. The entire life cycle is about three to four weeks.

The time to interrupt the life cycle is either before the adults have a chance to lay their eggs or before the eggs hatch. We tend to be generous with the water for our indoor plants, which provides ideal conditions for the gnats to breed. We need to learn to allow the medium in our pots to dry out to a depth of at least two to three inches (five to eight centimetres) before watering again. This creates inhospitable conditions for the gnats and is also better for plant health. To check the dryness of the soil, insert your finger into the soil. If it is still too wet, you will feel the damp on your finger. A ceramic mushroom can serve the same purpose. If the soil is damp, the unglazed "stem" will be discoloured at the bottom; if dry, the stem will be the same colour. We should also make a practice of removing the top two or three inches (five to eight centimetres) of growing medium every so often and replacing it with fresh medium.

Should you have an infestation, the first step is to create a barrier. I use a ¼-inch (6-millimetre) layer of play sand on top of the soil surface. This prevents the adults from laying their eggs since the larvae can't reach the surface of the soil. You can also use diatomaceous earth (DE), which acts to abrade the soft skins of the larvae, but do be sure to use food-grade DE.

Traps work to eliminate adults—either the yellow sticky strips or apple cider vinegar in a jar with a top that has holes punched in it, so the gnats get in but then are stuck inside. You can also trap larvae by placing thin slices of potato on the surface of the medium. For whatever weird reason, the larvae gravitate to the potato. When you lift the slices up the next day, there will be larvae on the bottoms. Just chuck it all out—potato and larvae and all. It's gross, but it works.

If things are really out of control, you can use a beneficial nematode (*Steinernema feltiae*). The nematodes come in a powder that can be diluted in water or on a sponge that can be immersed in water and squeezed to get the nematodes out. Whichever vehicle you choose, drench the plant when you water it with the nematode/water mixture. The nematodes will then enter the bodies of the larvae and release a bacterium, which will kill them. Not a cheap solution, but effective.

Other measures include Bti (*Bacillus thuringiensis* subsp. *israelensis*), which is often used in greenhouse operations. A diluted mixture of 3 percent hydrogen peroxide (one part peroxide to four parts water) is another option.

If absolutely everything you try doesn't manage the miracle of no fungus gnats in your home, there is one last thing to do. Just accept them as part of the price of being passionate about gardening![20]—JM

Is it more difficult to attract pollinator insects to plants if I live in a high-rise apartment? Can I do something to remedy this?

The bees, wasps, flies, butterflies, moths, and beetles that may pollinate your plants have specific needs: pollen, nectar, host plants to feed upon, and protected spots to lay their eggs. These may be difficult to fulfill on an apartment balcony, which can be windy, dry and hot, and fully exposed to the elements. On top of that, many pollinators such as bees and butterflies typically don't like to fly high—they tend to stick closer to the ground where food is more plentiful and it is less work to obtain.

While it is difficult to attract pollinators to such an unwelcome place, you can turn things around. Erect trellises or other structures to use as windbreaks—and be sure to plant them up with a flowering vine! Increasing the diversity of plants on your balcony will make a huge difference. Mix edible plants, such as scarlet runner beans, peas, and squash, with flowers and herbs, such as zinnias, parsley, nasturtiums, dill, lavender, calendulas, borage, oregano, thyme, and sweet peas.

Finally, if you really cannot seem to feel the love from the pollinators out there, you can always manually pollinate the plants that need it. Some gardeners use an artist's paintbrush or a cotton swab to gently transfer the pollen from flowers; sometimes, all the plant needs is a light shake of the stems to help things along.[21] —SN

If you are a balcony gardener, are there any special considerations or restrictions to know before planting?

Yes, there can be a whole lot to think about! You'll need to do your research. If you live in a condominium, it is imperative to consult your bylaws before you start buying any gardening supplies. Some condo boards will not allow a single container of plants on their balconies. Many rules have to do with safety concerns: window boxes, hanging baskets, and containers that are not properly secured may crash down into other units or onto passers-by during a windstorm. Other rules may govern sightlines. For example, you may not be able to have window boxes hanging off the balcony railing or the containers may have to be a certain colour. Setting up your four-shelf greenhouse on the balcony might violate a restriction that says you cannot have tall objects in that space.

Most importantly, consider the weight of containers, soil, and water. Your balcony may not be rated to support a large-scale gardening endeavour. If you overload your balcony, and a structural issue arises out of it, your insurance isn't likely to cover it. Finally, be cautious when you water—you don't want water dripping onto the balcony below you. Your neighbour isn't going to be pleased with you, and you may be reported. Be courteous and careful, and realize that your space is part of a community.

If you just purchased a home in a new urban development, you may have to think about a few of these things as well. Developers may restrict the species of trees and shrubs you can plant on your property or require that your containers are a certain colour. Know the rules before you plant, as it will save you a lot of grief later. —SN

Lettuce is a beautiful and delicious leafy crop that thrives in containers.

What are some fantastic plant selections for container gardening?

Choose the right plant for the site! Peruse these lists for the top selections to grow in containers.

VEGETABLES

All sorts of veggies grow well in containers! The trick is to choose smaller-sized varieties and to not skimp on the size of your container.

* Arugula
* Asian greens (bok choi, mizuna, and many more)
* Beans (pole and runner rather than bush types)
* Beets
* Carrots
* Cucumbers (slicing and pickling)

* Endive and escarole
* Kale
* Leeks
* Lettuce (Bibb, head, leaf, and romaine types)
* Onions (scallion and multiplier)
* Peas (snow and snap rather than shelling)
* Peppers (both hot and sweet)
* Potatoes (indeterminate varieties are best)
* Radishes
* Spinach
* Squash (smaller-sized fruit are best)
* Swiss chard
* Tomatoes (cherry, grape, and other small varieties)[22] —JM

Truthfully, it's like herbs were created for container growing. Experiment with these varieties and more! Aggressive spreaders such as mint are contained and manageable in pots instead of being allowed to roam freely all over the garden. You can also overwinter many of these herb plants indoors, so you don't have to replant every year.

* Anise hyssop
* Basil
* Borage
* Calendula
* Chamomile
* Chives
* Cilantro
* Dill
* Fennel
* Lavender

* Lemon balm
* Lemon verbena
* Marjoram
* Mint
* Oregano
* Rosemary
* Sage
* Tarragon
* Thyme
* Tulsi (holy basil)—SN

Highly attractive and useful as a culinary herb, rosemary has wide appeal.

EDIBLE FLOWERS

You have a huge range to choose from! Make sure your flowers are free from chemical residue and pollutants. Remember that some plants may cause allergic reactions and other health problems for some people, so do your research before you eat or feed others any of these blooms. Wash the flowers well before serving.

Calendula is also known as pot marigold, which refers to its use in cooking.

* Anise hyssop
* Basil
* Borage
* Calendula
* Chervil
* Chives
* Cilantro
* Dill
* Fennel
* Lavender
* Mint
* Nasturtium
* Pansy
* Scarlet runner bean
* Squash
* Violet

Finally, I have been asked several times over the years if sweet pea flowers are edible, and they absolutely are not. In fact, they are extremely toxic. —SN

HEAT- AND DROUGHT-TOLERANT ANNUALS

Just because these selections fare a bit better than others in exposed, hot, and dry conditions doesn't mean you can totally neglect them. They'll thrive and put on a reliable show for you if you give them a little TLC every once in a while.

* Ageratum
* Bougainvillea
* Geranium (including ivy-leaved and scented geraniums)
* Lantana
* Mandevilla
* Portulaca
* Sage
* Sunflower
* Sweet potato vine
* Verbena
* Zinnia

Don't forget sedums (stonecrops) and succulents! There are numerous species and cultivars to choose from, and they can add a huge amount of interest and texture to containers. —SN

The wow factor is strong with this succulent container!

FOLIAGE PLANTS

These are some perennials that can be planted into beds at the end of the season to overwinter:

* Bergenia
* Boxwood
* Coral bells
* Euonymus
* Golden creeping Jenny

* Hosta
* Periwinkle
* Yucca

ANNUALS (INCLUDING GRASSES)

Short-lived but stunning, these ornamental grasses and annual plants add texture and—in many cases—height to your containers.

* Coleus
* Corkscrew rush
* Fountain grass or purple fountain grass

* Golden millet 'Flashlights' grass
* Papyrus
* Sweet potato vine

HOUSEPLANTS THAT CAN DO DOUBLE DUTY OUTSIDE IN THE SUMMER

These popular houseplants will happily vacation outdoors in warm weather and add a lively spark of colour and texture to your containers. You'll get a sense of the tropics without taking a bite out of your plant budget!

* Asparagus fern
* Banana
* Boston fern
* Croton
* Elephant ear
* Inch plant
* Ivy

* Japanese painted fern
* Lily of the Nile (Agapanthus)
* Peacock plant
* Rex begonia[23]

—JM & SN

Raised Beds

2

What types of materials can I build raised beds from?

Go for it:

* Any untreated wood
* Vinyl
* Recycled plastic (for example, high-density polyethylene)
* Bricks, concrete blocks, poured concrete
* Steel
* Corrugated metal
* Rock
* Fabric (for example, polypropylene)

Avoid:

* Wood that was treated before 2004
* Treated pallets
* Tires

Wooden raised beds may be painted to complement the style of your home and garden. (The forks stuck in the soil are to deter unwanted animal pests such as squirrels and cats.)

Things to consider:

* Your budget
* Availability of materials
* Durability (some materials may rust, rot, or otherwise break down faster than others)
* Whether you want a prefabricated bed or you want to DIY
* Aesthetics (does the bed fit with your garden style?)
* Temperature variations (for example, beds made of metal may retain heat and cold more than other types of materials)
* Your personal opinions regarding use of manufactured materials (for example, plastics) versus natural ones, such as rock and wood. —SN

Untreated wood is a good option for raised-bed gardens for edibles

Here is a new take on "untreated" wood!

Using treated wood is a choice left to the gardener; it is not recommended to use old wood that was treated before 2004.

What about planting in galvanized troughs or stock tanks? Is it safe?

Galvanized troughs are commonly used as raised beds or planters, and it is fashionable to plant in galvanized pails and pots. Yes, they do contain zinc, and some people are worried about too much zinc from the containers leaching into the soil and, therefore, into our edible crops. Humans actually consume a certain amount of zinc on a daily basis from our food, and, if you think about it, those troughs were meant for livestock to drink out of regularly. Individual plants can take up only a very small amount of zinc from the containers, and we aren't at risk when we eat that produce. Use a food-grade plastic liner if you are concerned about safety.[1] —SN

Can I use pressure-treated wood to build raised beds?

Pressure-treated wood is made by combining high pressure with preservatives, which is then applied to the wood to strengthen its defences against rot. In Canada, wood used in residential building projects may be treated with preservation agents, such as alkaline copper quaternary (ACQ) and, to a lesser degree, copper azole (CA-B). The chromated copper arsenate (CCA) that was commonly employed years ago was phased out in 2004.

ACQ and CA-B are considerably less toxic than CCA—the lack of arsenic is an indicator. (Bear in mind that we actually have trace amounts of copper, arsenic, and chromium in our soils—they're naturally occurring.) They are much safer than the old-school treated wood, but whether or not you use them is definitely a choice you'll want to make for yourself.[2] Particulate copper preservative treatments are a recent introduction to the market. Instead of dissolving copper into a solvent—which is how ACQ is made—manufacturers grind copper into microscopic particles. When pressurized, the particles actually work themselves into the cells of the wood, instead of remaining on the surface. Voila—no leaching![3]—SN

What kinds of non-toxic, eco-friendly wood preservatives and stains can I use on my raised beds or wooden planters?

There are several to choose from, but bear in mind that most of them will not weather well without frequent reapplications. (Some may need to be brushed on at least twice a year.)

Beeswax, unsurprisingly, is quite water resistant.

Carnauba wax is made from a type of palm tree, and it's even more water resistant than beeswax.

Mineral oil is less water resistant than the waxes, but it is colourless, odourless, and tasteless (if that matters—it might, depending on what surface you're applying it to).

Raw linseed oil, made from flaxseeds, has an incredibly long curing time and must be reapplied frequently. Polymerized linseed oil (sometimes called stand oil) has a shorter curing time and is easy to apply.

Walnut oil must be reapplied often.

Tung oil has good water resistance, but you'll need to put on several coats to secure decent coverage.

Pine tar may be a bit unusual, but it has excellent water resistance.

Mixing mineral oil and beeswax increases the ease of application and water resistance.

There are some eco-friendly wood preservatives on the market made from various combinations of minerals; your local hardware store will be able to source these for you, if you're interested.[4]—SN

To extend the longevity of wooden planters, beds,
and boxes, apply a non-toxic preservative or stain.

Do I need to line my raised bed with anything, or put something down at the base when I am building it?

The short answer: it's complicated. You don't *need* a liner, but you may wish to have one.

Proponents of using a liner cite its usefulness in discouraging rodent pests from digging up a bed, as well as its value as a weed blocker. Some gardeners also feel that if no liner or base is used, there is a risk of the soil "escaping" out of the bottom of the bed. Others hope that a liner will help stave off rot in a raised bed made from wood that hasn't been sealed with a preservative. Alternatively, if wood is treated with chemicals that are not food safe, a liner is sometimes used in an attempt to prevent leaching. (This isn't always successful, so don't count on it. It's better to build your raised beds from materials that are not potentially harmful to human health.)

In addition to the pros, it's also important to weigh the cons of the materials commonly used as liners. Some do not allow for the necessary drainage. Some may be damaged by an errant stab from a garden fork as you work in the garden bed, or be chewed through by voles or mice. The lack of natural interface between the contents of the raised bed and the field soils beneath it may be something to think about. If your goal is to boost soil health and support the life within it, you may not want to put up a barricade.

Common materials used for liners include:

Plastic: Whether it's a polyethylene tarp or a pool liner, plastic is durable and dependable, but it usually does not promote drainage. Polypropylene sheets offer some permeability, and work somewhat better for drainage.

Landscape fabric (weed barrier): Every community garden I've ever been a member of has used this particular product in their raised beds. It is relatively inexpensive and allows for drainage. It also discourages weed growth. However, over the long term, it is not as durable as some other liners.

Canvas: Some gardeners prefer to use canvas as an alternative to landscape fabric, and it does have more longevity than a low-grade landscape fabric.

Hardware cloth: This is a good option, as it should last longer than the life of your bed, and rodents aren't likely to take it on at any point. It is also excellent for promoting drainage. However, as a weed barrier, it isn't as useful as the other options; although if you concoct a hardware cloth and fabric combination, you might have a winner.

As for a base for your raised bed, gravel is one of the most popular and inexpensive options. Wood chips may also be used. Some gardeners choose to lay down thick layers of newspaper or cardboard to kill the grass at the base, and top it off with a layer of organic materials, such as straw, twigs, leaves, and grass clippings. Others plan well in advance and use black plastic sheeting to smother the grass a few months before constructing the bed. Still others choose to dig out the grass instead of smothering it. Either way, bear in mind that perennial weeds may become an issue in the future if they are not thoroughly removed.

Your budget is also going to play a large role in your decision. Hardware cloth, for example, isn't cheap, and if you are lining many beds with it, you may not be terribly thrilled with the dent it makes in your wallet.

Bear in mind that no matter what you select as a bed liner or a base —or if you decide not to go with one at all —you'll still have to weed your raised bed at some point. Weed seeds may blow in from surrounding areas or be deposited by birds. As a gardener, the moment you accept that the potential for weeds is a constant, you'll feel much better about what can often feel like a futile endeavour.[5] —SN

How deep does a raised garden bed have to be?

If you are going to be sowing only shallow-rooted veggies like leafy greens, six inches (fifteen centimetres) of soil is sufficient. But, as you are already expending the labour and money to construct a raised bed, why not make it suitable for deeper-rooted vegetables, so that if you decide to grow tomatoes, carrots, or parsnips in the future, they will have the space they need? Aim for a minimum of twelve inches (thirty centimetres)—more is even better!—and you'll be covered for everything.—SN

When constructing a raised bed, go big on the depth. This gives you the ability to grow plants with deep roots.

What is a wicking bed? How do I create one?

Wicking beds are designed to sub-irrigate the soil, which simultaneously conserves water and ensures that the soil is consistently moist for optimum plant growth. They are self-contained beds with a reservoir of water situated beneath the soil. This allows for water to be "wicked up" via capillary action through the soil to become available to plants.

Wicking beds are more expensive and take longer than your average raised bed to build. The frame of the bed may be constructed from any materials used for raised beds, although wood and metal are the most common. Line the bed with a sturdy, durable black pond liner. Install a PVC pipe at a height of eight inches (twenty centimetres) for use as an overflow pipe by drilling through the liner and the frame.

Then, lay down weeping tile or PVC piping with holes drilled in it through the length of the bed and attach it to an L-shaped inlet PVC pipe that is at least three inches (eight centimetres) in diameter. Add gravel, scoria (coarse red volcanic rock), or other material to cover the weeping tile. Overtop this layer, place geotextile fabric, which will stop the soil above from seeping into the reservoir. If using a wooden frame, I usually staple the fabric in place, so that it doesn't shift. Finally, in goes the soil mix, and you are good to go.

Beds can be made for any soil depth above the base layer, with the average being two to three feet (sixty to ninety centimetres). Any taller and the force of gravity will take over and moisture will not reach the top layer. In windy areas I find that lower beds are better since the wind can evaporate soil moisture faster than the capillary action can work, though mulching reduces surface evaporation considerably.

Wicking beds can be a good solution for any area where there is a hard surface or contaminated soil. They are also excellent for gardeners who cannot readily attend to their beds since water use is about half that of a regular bed. I always recommend a wicking bed if you want to site a raised bed near trees, especially spruce and poplar, that will reach out to your bed for moisture and nutrients. The best plant selections for wicking beds are annuals, particularly edibles, as

This overhead view displays the sub-irrigation system in a wicking bed.

These wicking beds have a vertical component with the addition of trellises.

perennials will establish large root systems that can invade the geotextile fabric overtop, right into the reservoir. An additional benefit is that less fertilizer is often required, in particular nitrogen, as it is retained in the system.

On the other hand, wicking beds are not for everyone or all situations. The expense is a definite deterrent, and they use a lot of manufactured materials. The other drawback is the way they work. Given that the soil is perched on the water below, the bottom layer is always on the wet side, so deep-rooting plants can suffer from root rot and other conditions. Additionally, the wicking action brings salts up to the top surface, due to their inability to leach out of the bed.[6]—JM

What types of soil mixes should be used in raised beds?

The ideal soil mixes for raised beds will vary and are dependent on several factors. The size of the bed matters as well as how deep it is because the soil can both dry out faster in raised beds and compact under its own weight. Whether the bed is open at the bottom, so that there is an interface with the underlying native soil, or sealed makes a difference, too. The native soil, whether it is heavily clay-based or tending toward sandy, as well as the natural pH of the soil, will need to be factored in. Finally, weather can influence the composition of the mix you want—for example, windy areas will dry out or erode soil in raised beds faster.

The goal is a soil mix that is easy to cultivate and has good moisture retention but is also well-draining, with good aeration. Ideally, the pH factor should be neutral to slightly acidic, especially if annual edibles are the dominant plants. The soil should be highly fertile since the nutrients in raised beds are consumed very quickly. The mix should be hospitable to and support a diverse soil life. To boot, it should be weed-free. In short, we want the holy grail of soil that all gardeners aspire to—whether it is in-ground, mounded, or in raised beds: loam!

I am a bit of a (okay, really off-the-scale) fanatic about getting the soil for a raised bed right the first time, as the work and time to remediate poor soil is massive. I never recommend filling a bed with overturned grass sod unless it is guaranteed to be weed-free. (I especially want to avoid quack grass.) Nor do I recommend relying solely on commercial soil mixes since they have standardized proportions, rather than being tailored for your specific needs. The last thing I want is to have the bulk of the soil dumped in the bed and then have to amend it.

Use these steps to fill a brand new bed with the dimensions of 8 feet (2.4 metres) by 4 feet (1.2 metres) by 2 feet (0.6 metres), which is 64 cubic feet or 1.8 cubic metres:

Place a large tarp on the ground beside the bed. You will use it to work your mix together.

These brand new raised beds are filled with a high-quality soil mix.

I am not the sort of person who measures or follows recipes, but what I start with is 35 cubic feet (1 cubic metre) of a top-quality soil mix from someone I know and trust. It is important to learn as much as you can about the mix you are using. Know the proportions of the components, where they came from, how they were used previously, and how long the mix has been aging. The mix must be free of pesticides and weeds, especially perennial weeds. The proportions and components in mixes vary. A garden mix can include any of the following: topsoil, peat moss, compost, manure, and perlite in various amounts. At a minimum, use a mix with 50 percent topsoil, 25 to 30 percent peat moss, and 20 to 25 percent compost.

To that mix, I add 17.5 cubic feet (0.5 cubic metres) of compost. Then in goes a big bag of perlite for aeration and water retention. I avoid vermiculite if the topsoil is likely to be heavy.

To increase soil fertility, I add worm compost, fish meal, kelp or alfalfa meal, and volcanic rock dust that contains a multitude of trace minerals, useful for

Using top-notch planting media can help you create a highly successful raised-bed garden!

healthy plants (I swear by it!). I finish it off with a dollop of inert mycorrhizal fungi. If possible, I also use a microbial extract made from worm compost, as it contains water-soluble nutrients and microbes and greatly aids in establishing the soil biology of the bed.

Now I can plant! I know my soil will provide the best environment for a productive first year. At the end of the season, before winter sets in, I add more compost and nutrients, so that they have a chance to settle into the bed for next year's planting. This is especially important if you're growing edibles.[7] —JM

Do I have to worry that the soil in my planter boxes is right up against the siding of my home?

This could prove to be an issue over the long term. Constant moisture from the soil can promote mould, mildew, and rot; it may even invite pest insects to take up residency in that location. Installation of a waterproof membrane between the soil and the wall may help, as long as the barrier remains intact. Your very best bet, however, is to leave a gap between the planter and the exterior wall, so that the soil cannot touch the siding. Ensure your planter box has sufficient drainage and that the water runs away from the house. —SN

What is square foot gardening? How does it work?

Square foot gardening is an iconic planting method that dates back to the 1970s.

Mel Bartholomew, an American engineer, analyzed the backyard vegetable gardens at the time and determined that they were largely wasteful of resources, created extra work, and were not all that productive for the amount of space they utilized. As a teenager deployed during summer holidays to weed our large vegetable garden, I can attest to the work involved!

In response, Bartholomew proposed a system based on four principles that employ much less space and are incrementally more productive. By revising the geometry of the garden, he determined that the square foot (12 inches by 12 inches/30 centimetres by 30 centimetres) would become the foundation of his new system, and that the optimum size of a bed should be no more than 4 feet by 4 feet (1.2 metres by 1.2 metres). Those specific dimensions reflect his observation that the average person can comfortably reach 2 feet (60 centimetres) into a bed to tend or harvest edibles without needing to plant one's foot in the bed. Ideally, the beds can be raised, 6 to 12 inches (15 to 30 centimetres) deep, to keep the volume of soil down.

Bartholomew also suggested that pathways be created around each bed to provide easy access on all sides. These easy-to-tend pathways can be made of grass, gravel, or wood chip mulch. Immediate benefits then accrue as the pathways are permanent, using materials other than garden soil and not requiring mitigation of compacted soil.

The second square foot gardening principle involves using each square foot to guide placement of seeds or seedlings. A solid grid of square feet is placed on top of the soil, and the gardener then sows within each square. (I advise making the grid out of wood or metal. String or other more flexible materials offer the temptation to push the sides in just a little to fit one more seed in. I know because I have done it!)

Bartholomew worked out how many squares each type of common edible would require for optimum growth and harvest. For instance, the small-footprint edibles

*This freshly planted bed
has been gridded for
square foot gardening.*

such as carrots and leeks can be sown or transplanted in a grid of four by four within one square. Lettuce, kale, and chard can also be assigned a grid of four by four seeds per seedlings per square. Slightly larger plants such as spinach, beets, and bush beans can be allotted nine plants per square. Still larger plants such as cabbage, broccoli, peppers, and potatoes are apportioned one plant per square. Each tomato plant takes up four squares! The benefits to following these rules include planting less seed and reducing work, as you don't need to thin the extra seedlings.

The third principle focuses on the growing medium for the beds. Bartholomew created Mel's Mix, which calls for one-third peat moss, one-third vermiculite, and one-third compost. It is a very light medium, which holds moisture well and does not compact easily. The benefits include less work preparing the soil for the bed and a medium that warms up quickly in spring and is weed-free to start off. Having used this recipe and being a self-confessed soil groupie, I find that this mix doesn't cut it for our prairie conditions. It has little substance to it, dries out easily, and has little to offer the plants growing in it. There simply isn't enough complexity to the mix for optimal growing. I prefer taking the time to remove whatever is underneath the bed, so that the bed is situated on top of the underlying soil. Over time the growing medium in the bed will integrate readily with the soil biology and nutrients below. There won't be a hard interface, so that water can move through the layers easily. Through trial and error, the mix that I have come to rely on for our prairie conditions includes some of the native soil in the garden, peat moss, perlite, and lots of compost, along with fertilizers (see pages 82–84). You'll know when you have got it right—when what you are using has a good feel, smell, and look to it.

There is plenty of room in a square foot for these beautiful lettuce seedlings.

The fourth principle is about watering. To avoid wasting water, Bartholomew advocates hand-watering each plant, using a bucket of rainwater and a dipper so that the action of watering is deliberate and controlled. All plants can then receive optimal moisture for the stage of growth that they are at. Plus, when you are hand-watering, you are looking at your plants and can easily spot potential problems or spy that first ripe cherry tomato. Bartholomew later included the option of drip irrigation for watering and mulching to conserve soil moisture.

I recommend the square foot system for most common edibles and annual flowers, but not for perennials, as the space and resources they require is out of proportion for a small bed. When using this system, I tend to go more with smaller edibles, such as greens, root veggies, and herbs. The bigger plants tend to take up more than their allotted space. Square foot gardening also lends itself neatly to companion planting and interplanting, which increases productivity.

When designing your bed, think outside the box. Consider whether you would like one end deeper than the other. Or perhaps design the bed as a keyhole shape for better access to the middle. Do you need to stand to garden? If so, a tabletop bed can be a square foot bed.

Square foot gardening as a design and planting system works well, especially for new gardeners. I use the system a lot in my teaching and horticultural therapy programs, as it is easy to learn and follow. In my own garden I am not so rigid with the planting guidelines, as I like to do a lot of interplanting, but the underlying principles are bang on. Your imagination is the only limitation, and the end result should be exactly what works best for your garden and you. Enjoy gardening so that it is never a chore![8] —JM

What is lasagna gardening? How can it be used in raised beds?

Lasagna gardening has been around since 1999, when Patricia Lanza's book of the same name caused a stir in the gardening world. It is another name for sheet mulching or sheet composting, which has been a staple of permaculture since the 1970s, although the basic technique has been practised for centuries. Lasagna gardening is an apt name for it, though, because it evokes the many layers that are involved.

The essence of this style of gardening is the creation of a garden bed by cold composting in place, which eliminates digging out the underlying surface, typically grass or perhaps a hardscrabble area. It works on hard surfaces, such as pavement or gravel, or even a rooftop.

To start, define the area that will be the bed. Then lay down a layer of cardboard, newspaper, or burlap to suppress and ultimately kill the plants already there by denying them oxygen and light. Water it thoroughly. The next layer of about four inches (ten centimetres) is composed of twigs, small branches, tough stalks from perennial plants, and so on. This layer is there to provide drainage for the bed, especially when everything starts to settle and degrade. Water this layer thoroughly.

Then layer compost, manure, yard waste, and kitchen scraps about two inches (five centimetres) deep, topped off with a good eight inches (twenty centimetres) of straw or dried leaves. Water the layers again. Keep repeating the layers until the bed is as high as you want it, allowing for it to settle over time. At this point, you can stop and let nature take its course and come back after a few months to top the bed off with another layer or more of some of the above materials, depending on how much it has sunk. But if you want to plant into it right away, then move to the final step and top the bed off with a good six inches (fifteen centimetres) of garden soil.

Limit plants in the first season to those with shallow and fibrous root systems. Annual vegetables and flowers are perfect. The layers underneath will be taking their time to degrade and will slowly become a nutrient-rich and easy-to-work bed.

After the first season, the layers will have compressed significantly. Be prepared to add further layers to bring it back up to the desired height, topping it off with another layer of garden soil each season until it stabilizes.

A mounded lasagna bed can look somewhat rough and ready, but the method can be easily done as a raised bed. I would recommend laying down the first layer of cardboard with extra on each side, then building your frame overtop. Then layer the lasagna materials inside the frame. The cardboard on the outside will deter grass from growing up inside the bed.

As with everything, there are pros and cons to lasagna gardening. It certainly is cost effective as it avoids having to bring in loads of garden soil and uses a lot of recycled materials. The soil that is created over time is truly fertile, with a terrific soil biology, and a dream to work with. The downside is the amount of materials you need to have on hand to get started. It is really not practical to attempt to build a really large lasagna garden, but it is a great method for a small garden or a raised bed. Plus, as with cold composting, it does take time for the layers to "cook" and blend together. The earthworms have a lot of work to do! There is the potential for weeds from all those materials, and pests can be attracted to the decomposing layers. Another worry is that perennial weeds, such as quack grass, which can grow through anything, may become a maintenance problem.[9]—JM

What is a hügelkultur bed?

I am a big hügelkultur fan! I have incorporated these beds into many gardens I have worked on, including my own.

As with much in gardening, we reach back to the past for some of our best practices, and hügelkultur or mound/hill culture is one of them. It is raised-bed gardening at its simplest. In a world where waste materials should be upcycled rather than discarded, the idea is that you collect the old rotting deadfall, untreated lumber scraps, and miscellaneous branches and twigs that won't readily compost and pile them to form a mound in the size and shape you want. I prefer not to use sod as it often contains quack grass. Climb on top of it and stomp around to compress it, if you like, then add more woody materials until you get to the height you want, plus a bit more. Most hügelkultur beds are around three feet (one metre) high, but I have seen them upwards of six feet (two metres). Talk about vertical gardening!

Then pile on dried leaves, manure, straw, and compost that hasn't quite decomposed to settle in between the wood layers. Water the pile well, so that if you pick up a handful, it feels spongy and wet. Add more dry materials, alternating with watering, until you have a nice mound. Finally, add a layer of finished compost and garden soil to the mound, then water again. You can build your bed in the fall and allow it to settle further over the winter or go ahead and plant it right away, so long as you understand that the soil biology and physical properties are very "raw" at first. If you plant in the hügelkultur bed immediately, it is recommended that any sort of legumes be the first crop as they are nitrogen fixers and won't suffer as the soil biology kicks in.

So, what are the benefits accruing from all this work?

To start with, the planting area in a hügelkultur bed is much more expansive than a traditional bed as all sides as well as the top are used for plants, so they are great for small garden spaces. What fascinates me though is what happens inside the bed. The core of the bed, being wood, will start to decay as the soil microbes multiply, releasing nutrients for plants to take up over the years. The soil biology is fantastic with microbes, insects, and other organisms involved. The mound is well aerated as the various materials break down, which means that there is no need to till. The magic though is how the whole mound becomes a moisture reservoir, which reduces the need for watering. Snowmelt and rainfall will keep the mound moist, and the plants will develop deep roots and be drought resistant. Plus, the decaying wood will give out gentle heat, which provides temperature modification during cooler nights and can extend the growing season. The mound heats up earlier too, so you can get started planting earlier in the season. Hügelkultur gardening is much easier on the body since much can be done standing up. Lastly, there is considerable carbon sequestration in a hügelkultur bed, and the technique uses materials that often go to the landfill.

Over time, the bed will reduce in size, and you can simply top it up with more compost and soil to keep it at the height you want. At some point you may decide to take it apart and start anew, using the remains of the old one as the "mother" for the new one, just like the process for baking sourdough bread!

Some people will frame in their beds with pallets and other found materials. Others might enclose them with wood or stone to make them more pleasing to their eyes, but that does reduce the planting area. I have even built raised beds that need to be enclosed to make them accessible and built the hügelkultur from within.

Hügelkultur beds are versatile, too. They can be used for edibles, including herbs, vegetables, and fruit shrubs. They can be a perennial bed, a pollinator garden, a food forest, a pumpkin patch, or a corn hill. Formal, informal, fancy or not, you get to make the choices. I have even seen one that was made into a Hobbit hill, à la *The Lord of the Rings*.[10] —JM

Small Plots and Postage Stamp–Sized Yards

3

What are microclimates? How can I use them to my advantage in my small-space garden?

Large rocks are used to create a microclimate for this fernleaf peony.

If climate represents the weather conditions for an area in general, then micro-climates are those small variations of weather within your garden. The growing conditions will be slightly or even profoundly different from those not too far away. A microclimate can be 2 square feet (0.19 square metres) or almost the area encompassing a whole garden. One of my smallest microclimates is a mounded bed right under the dryer vent. Guess where the first crocus always pops up?

With microclimates, many factors come into play, from the orientation of the garden from north to east, and shading from buildings or large trees during the day, depending on what the season is, to the colour and materials of surrounding buildings and the slope of the garden; from low and higher spots and drier or wetter soil, to different kinds of soil; from overhanging eaves, to the way the wind comes across and around the garden. The list is endless, and the average garden may have many microclimates. More importantly, you can create or mitigate microclimate conditions to suit what you are growing.

The first step is to learn what sort of microclimates you have already and the impact they have on what is in the garden. Walk around your garden and feel where the breeze comes from; observe where there is shade during what times of the day. How does the sun, as it shifts through the sky, as the season progresses, affect light versus shade? Where are the hot and cool spots and the high and low ones? Are there areas that are always dry or wet, and why? What is your soil's texture and structure? What structures are there that make a difference, and how?

It is a process that takes time. I usually give myself at least three years before I feel like I know the microclimates in any given garden, especially as things keep changing with trees being taken out, patios being built, and so forth. When I took out a deck and replaced it with a brick patio, I sure learned that in a hurry!

Then plant your garden with those variables in mind. Grapes should go in that southwest-facing nook that collects all the warmth of the sun. There is no point in planting squash in the lowest part of the garden. They will never ripen before the first frosts, and they will come there first. Windy areas will dry out beds faster. Shade is best left to woodland plants since roses need direct sun to bloom. Full-on sun will scorch tomatoes and thin the leaves of lettuces, but yarrow and gas plant adore it. Onion bulbs will rot in cold, wet, and heavy soil. It is all knowledge gained through observation and experience. I once put a nice brick edge to a pathway and promptly changed the direction water flowed during a storm and nearly washed away a bed of lettuce.

What I love doing is purposefully changing the microclimates in my gardens to create better growing conditions and overall garden resiliency in our changing climate. Raised beds will warm up faster in the spring than in-ground ones. Even a low raised bed of six inches (fifteen centimetres) will be enough to make a difference. If it is an annual bed, covering it with black plastic at the end of the season will serve to warm up the soil earlier come spring to get you planting faster.

Use brick, wood, cement, and stones because they warm up during the day and release that heat overnight, moderating temperatures and allowing plants to keep growing without pause. Deploy containers of water to provide the same benefit for those warm-season crops, such as tomatoes and peppers, that are so sensitive to cooler temperatures.

Trellises can be erected to cut the sun's intensity and to redirect winds. If positioned strategically, they can also serve to protect plants from hail. A stand of sunflowers can do the same thing. Putting shade cloth overtop of beds of lettuce and spinach will lengthen the harvest.

Using polytunnels and cold frames over beds will create their own special microclimates and protect against hail. Positioning a floating row cover over an edible bed all season long will cut the intensity of our sun, trap some humidity within the enclosed space, moderate air and soil temperatures, conserve soil moisture, and more. Plants will be succulent, tastier, and more productive.

Temporary buffers can be employed by strategically placing garden furniture, portable screens, and artwork. Adding a pond or a fountain will add humidity to the surrounding air.

Plants also can create microclimates, especially if using companion planting and interplanting techniques to utilize the physical properties of plants. Cabbage plants with their big leaves can shelter a newly emerging crop of spinach, providing an environment that is cooler and slightly more humid for the seedlings to enjoy. Mulching keeps the soil cool and moist and the plants healthy, so they can "weather" the weather better.

There are so many techniques and tricks to take advantage of microclimates, and we are learning new ones all the time. It's fun inventing ones too, so long as we work within what is possible and not hanker to create a microclimate way outside the parameters of our region's overall climate. I am not sure that we will be growing bananas outside any time soon![1] —JM

This interplanting of broccoli and lettuce is an example of plants forming microclimates to benefit each other.

What is a grafted tree and how can they be useful in a small garden?

Grafting is a method of vegetatively joining two—and sometimes more—plants together. One plant provides the roots and the trunk and is appropriately called the rootstock. A shoot from another plant serves as the upper portion of the plant and is called a scion. Scions are usually selected for special traits such as flavourful fruit, colourful flowers or foliage, or disease resistance. Roots and scions should be close relatives. The knobby location where they are joined is called the graft union.

One of the most popular reasons to graft trees is to create dwarf specimens that are suitable for small yards. Combining the rootstock of a dwarf tree with a desirable scion may give you that small fruit tree you really want—one that is easy to harvest and produces fruit faster than if you were to plant a tree that was not grafted.

One thing to watch out for when considering a grafted tree for your yard or garden is to ensure that the graft union is not buried beneath the soil. One of two things can occur if this happens: either your rootstock will begin sprouting its own top growth, or the scion will begin rooting. Up or down, you'll destroy the reason why the graft was done in the first place.[2]—SN

Do combination fruit trees and shrubs do well on the prairies?

Yes! Just ensure the rootstock and the scions are all hardy to whatever hardiness zone you are planting them in. Combination fruit trees and shrubs are highly useful in small yards, where you may not have room to plant cross-pollinator varieties. And what a treat to have several different cultivars of fruit to choose from—on one plant!

When purchasing a combination fruit tree, make sure the graft unions are healthy. They should be well calloused where they are joined. There should be no cracks or decay around the union, and the rootstock should not be forming suckers. —SN

Apples are popular candidates for multi-grafting.

101

What does it mean to espalier a fruit tree?
Why is this a good thing to do in a small garden?

*Apples and pears are excellent candidates
for espaliering on the prairies.*

Espaliering is the practice of systematically training trees or shrubs into a two-dimensional plane. The word is French, derived from the Italian *spalliera*, which literally means something to lean one's *spalla* (shoulder) against. This really describes what an espaliered tree does.

Espaliering is a very old horticultural practice, dating back to ancient Rome. In medieval times, the desire to have fruiting trees growing inside the safety of the castle or the manor walls, but needing a way to reduce the space fruit trees required, turned the practice into high art. Now that many of us have smaller gardens, the practice is steadily undergoing a revival.

A tree or shrub grown as an espalier takes up a fraction of the space a typical tree or shrub does and can be just as productive. Taking advantage of a wall can also provide real growth benefits since heat is absorbed during the day and released at night to moderate our cooler overnight temperatures. Harvesting is easier as the fruit is presented to you rather than you having to climb, stretch, and clamber to get at it. Espaliered trees and shrubs can also add to your garden aesthetic because they can be trained into beautiful shapes.

The cordon is the simplest shape with branches extending horizontally on either side from the trunk. The next simplest is the fan, where the branches are angled diagonally upward, creating a fan shape. The candelabra is like a cordon, but the ends of the branches turn upwards. Others can be lattice shaped. The possibilities for other shapes are endless.

Espaliering requires essential know-how and the commitment to continually train and prune your tree. Plants have minds of their own and will always want to grow three-dimensionally, so besides the major elements, there will be ongoing pruning to eliminate suckers and branches that want to grow outside of the design, plus you will want to nurture all the fruiting spurs. This is a long-term project, and patience is definitely a virtue!

To get started, build the basic frame. You will need two sturdy posts, set 8 feet (2.4 metres) apart. To create the trellis, at 18 inches (45 centimetres) from the ground, string 12-gauge wire between the posts. Then add additional wire spaced every 18 inches (45 centimetres) to the top of the posts.

Then select your plant, which ideally is a "whip"—a tree seedling no more than 3 feet (1 metre) tall, without any side branching. If you do not have access to a whip, then choose a once-to-two-year-old sapling that is grafted to a dwarf rootstock. You don't want your espalier to grow to a full-sized tree, nor do you want to choose older saplings where the branches have already solidified into their permanent shape.

Plant your whip or sapling in the middle of the trellis. If you have a whip, you will need to prune it down to the first growing point or bud that is roughly level with the first lateral wire.

If you are planting a sapling with multiple branches, plant it with two branches level with that first lateral wire. Tie the branches to the wire with foam wire ties. (If the branches are already formed, it may take a season or two to train them to be lateral.) Then remove the leader (middle stem) and any remaining branches. Ouch!

Through the season, remove any suckers that are growing straight up from the lateral branches. (If they are small enough, they can be rolled off with your thumb.) But do leave the short stubby branches that will be fruit bearing.

In the meantime, another leader will start growing at the main stem. Allow it to grow up to the next lateral wire, and then repeat the process. It will take five to seven years to grow and train your tree into its mature shape, which will be between 6 and 8 feet tall (2 to 2.4 metres). While it is growing, remove all the flowers each year as you do not want the tree to devote energy to fruit production. It hurts, but it is essential so that the tree develops properly. Continue to remove suckers, and prune spurs to be every 6 inches (15 centimetres) apart for optimum fruit production. Once your tree has reached the height and width you desire, then allow fruit production to commence.

Typically, harvests are equal to those of full-sized trees because of the training and fostering of spurs. Your job for subsequent years is to keep pruning to retain the shape of the tree, care for the fruit spurs, and ultimately enjoy your espaliered tree!

Suitable trees for espaliering are apple, pear, and plum. Sour cherry would be fun to try, and small fruit shrubs, such as saskatoons, are a possibility. Bear in mind that apple, pear, and plum trees need cross-pollination to bear fruit, so you may need to have a second tree of a different variety nearby.

Are you up for the challenge?[3] —JM

What are some ideal trees for small yards?

Trees suitable for a large garden look outsize and out of proportion in small-space gardens. They also take up so much room that there is no space left for anything else!

These days plant breeders are actively addressing this problem with cultivars of trees that we know work beautifully within the constraints of a smaller garden area. Typically, small-space trees are either columnar or pyramidal, weeping, or just plain small species that have the "normal" shape of a tree, just on a smaller scale, whether that pertains to its height or breadth.

Japanese tree lilac cultivar 'Ivory Silk' has highly fragrant blooms and a small stature.

DECIDUOUS

* Amur maple (*Acer ginnala*)
* Columnar Norway maple (*Acer platanoides* 'Columnare')
* Crimson Sentry Norway maple (*Acer platanoides* 'Crimson Sentry')
* Dakota Pinnacle birch (*Betula platyphylla*)
* Dreamweaver columnar crabapple (*Malus* × 'Dreamweaver')
* Dwarf Korean lilac (top-grafted) (*Syringa meyeri* 'Palibin' TG)
* Emerald Spire columnar crabapple (*Malus* × 'Jefgreen', 'Emerald Spire')
* Evans sour cherry (*Prunus cerasus* 'Evans')
* Ivory Silk Japanese tree lilac (*Syringa reticulata* 'Ivory Silk')
* Muckle plum (*Prunus* × *nigrella* 'Muckle')
* Parkland Pillar birch (*Betula platyphylla* 'Jefpark')
* Pin cherry (*Prunus pensylvanica*)
* Prairie Skyrise trembling aspen (*Populus tremuloides* 'Prairie Skyrise')
* Princess Kay plum (*Prunus nigra* 'Princess Kay')
* Purple Spire columnar crabapple (*Malus* × 'Jefspire', 'Purple Spire')
* Pyramidal mountain ash (*Sorbus aucuparia* 'Fastigiata')
* Regal Prince oak (*Quercus* × *warei* 'Regal Prince')
* River birch (*Betula nigra*)
* Rosthern Siberian crabapple (*Malus baccata* 'Rosthern')
* Royal Beauty weeping flowering crabapple (*Malus* × 'Royal Beauty')
* Sour cherry (Romance series)
* Sutherland caragana (*Caragana arborescens* 'Sutherland')
* Swedish columnar aspen (*Populus tremula* 'Erecta')
* Walker weeping caragana (top-grafted) (*Caragana arborescens* 'Walker' TG)
* Weeping caragana (top-grafted) (*Caragana arborescens* 'Pendula' TG)

❋ Cedar (*Thuja* spp.—any species and variety except
for 'Brandon')

❋ Columnar blue spruce (*Picea pungens* 'Fastigiata')

❋ Columnar Norway spruce (*Picea abies* 'Cupressina',
'Christina', 'Pyramidalis')

❋ Columnar Scots pine (*Pinus sylvestris* 'Fastigiata')

❋ Columnar white pine (*Pinus strobus* 'Fastigiata')

❋ Upright junipers (*Juniperus scopulorum* 'Wichita Blue',
'Moonglow', 'Medora', 'Cologreen')

❋ Weeping larch (*Larix decidua* 'Pendula')

❋ Weeping Norway spruce (*Picea abies* 'Pendula')

❋ Weeping white spruce (*Picea glauca* 'Pendula')[4]—JM

*Dwarf sour cherry trees are perfect
for small gardens—plus, they bear
delicious fruit!*

Which plants perform well when planted beneath coniferous and deciduous trees?

If you're a perennial, annual flowering plant, or ground cover, you're going to have a very difficult time competing against a tree when it comes to receiving sufficient water, nutrients, and light. Trees simply hog everything and you're left, quite literally, in the dust.

It is less challenging to plant beneath deciduous trees than coniferous ones—the latter tend to have dense lower branches and drop massive piles of needles and cones. (The autumn leaf drop of deciduous trees is generally easier for the gardener to clean up.) I recommend using containers filled with shade-loving annual plants around coniferous trees—it's an easy solution to an annoying problem, and you can change up the colours and cultivars of the container plants every growing season for a fresh new display.

The following plants will work best under deciduous trees, but if you want to experiment, try some of them beneath conifers. Do your research before you head out to the garden centre, as some of these plants are spreading ground covers and others may reseed freely if not deadheaded.

ANNUALS

* Begonia
* Coleus
* Impatiens
* Pansy

PERENNIALS

* Bergenia
* Bugleweed
* Catnip
* Columbine
* Coral bells
* Ferns (look for species that are rated to your hardiness zone)
* Hosta
* Irish moss
* Lamium (dead nettle)
* Lungwort
* Scotch moss
* Solomon's seal

Spring-flowering geophytes (bulbs), such as tulips, daffodils, crocuses, scillas, and grape hyacinths, may also be valuable choices for early season colour.

When planting beneath trees, ensure that you do not disturb the tree roots. Digging too deeply near them may cause injury. As well, do not pile too much fresh new soil on top of the existing tree roots, as rot may occur. Use just enough soil to properly plant the selections you've chosen for the site.

Keep up with supplementary irrigation and a consistent fertilizing schedule to ensure the health of your planted specimens. An application of mulch may be useful to help conserve moisture—but beware of mulch volcanoes. Too much mulch can be detrimental to the tree roots, even promoting rot.—SN

What is catch cropping and how is it useful in small gardens?

Catch cropping is a great way to maximize yields in a small garden. It's as easy as selecting a few quick-maturing "catch" plants, such as lettuce, arugula, scallions, radishes, or Asian greens, and tucking them into spaces adjacent to a larger, slower-growing crop. You will harvest the catch crops before the other plants grow in, so you won't have to worry too much that the catch crops will become heavily shaded or will get crowded by the longer-maturing crops. If you plant your veggies in rows, you have space for a catch crop or several, perhaps—just use the rows! Even in containers, you can always plunk a few lettuce seeds around your tomatoes and have fresh baby leaves before your tomatoes become full-sized.

Occasionally, you'll come across a reference to catch crops and their use as consolation plantings, if the main crop has failed. For example, if you lose all of your corn to a devastating hailstorm, and after you've removed the damaged plants, you can sow a quick-growing catch crop to fill the space and at least salvage something out of the season.

If you're looking to improve your soil instead of eating your catch crops, you can grow green manures, which are later chopped down and incorporated into the soil to add organic matter. Some green manures, such as peas, alfalfa, and lentils, are nitrogen-fixing. That means their roots have a symbiotic relationship with bacteria that are capable of removing nitrogen from the air and converting it to a usable form. The bacteria share their stores of nitrogen with the plants, which use it to grow. Ultimately, when green manures are dug into the soil, the nitrogen becomes available to other plants.[5] —SN

How does succession planting work, and how is it used to advantage in small-space gardens?

Radishes are a fast-growing crop commonly grown in succession.

Succession planting refers to two main methods of sowing seed, via staggered planting or a practice called "pick and sow." With staggered planting, you make several small plantings of the same crop at specific, scheduled times—usually three to four weeks apart, but it depends on how much space you have in your garden, the maturity rate of the crop, and how much you are looking to harvest of a certain crop. You may not want hundreds of radishes at once, just because they grow quickly. Instead, you can successively grow several crops. Another way to stagger your plantings is by growing more than one variety of the same type of crop, with each variety having a different maturity rate. If you plant 'Jack Be Little' pumpkins at 95 days and 'Howden' pumpkins at 115 days, then you'll be harvesting at different times. (Granted, you'll also be harvesting radically different-sized fruit!)

If you choose the pick-and-sow method, you'll grow one crop to harvest and pick it, then plant another crop in the exact same space. The crops can be the same type of plant or different. This works really well if you're juggling between cool- and warm-season crops, depending on the time of year, and it's a boon if you are really limited on space. Remember, you can plant crops in succession in raised beds, containers, or in-ground beds—anywhere you want to maximize space. You don't have to direct sow all of the crops either. If you have the ability to start some of them indoors using grow lights, you can certainly get a leg up on the whole process.

Successive gardening success (see what I did there?) rests on timing. You need to be aware of your area's frost-free period, so you know how much time you have to make your plantings. Also be sure to note how long it takes for each crop to germinate, grow, and reach maturity. Yes, a bit of mathematics is in order—but it's not difficult. It helps to draw up a spreadsheet or a list of your planting schedule before the season starts. Do it as you browse the seed catalogues and place your orders. That way you won't get partway through the growing season and forget what you were trying to accomplish. Once you've tried succession planting for a few years, you're bound to be so pleased with how it works that you won't ever go back!—SN

What does the term "underplanting" mean? How can it maximize space in my garden?

If you are growing a tall aspen tree, and you decide to plant a red currant plant at its base, then add a couple of lovely hostas beneath the currant, you've just accomplished a multi-storey underplanting. In a vegetable garden, an example of an underplanting might be some leaf lettuce tucked in beneath trellised zucchini or pattypan squash plants. No space is wasted with underplanting, but you do have to ensure that each plant participant has enough room to thrive and reach its maximum height and spread. Consider, as well, that each plant will be competing with the others for sunlight, nutrients, and water, so carefully determine compatibility before you plant. Typically, your understorey plants are going to be shade lovers. As well, remember that conifers don't tend to play nicely with most understorey plants; this type of planting generally works better with deciduous trees.

Bear in mind that you will have to keep up with supplemental watering and fertilizing when needed. —SN

What is straw bale gardening? How is it useful in small spaces?

Straw bale gardening is exactly as the name describes: you plop a straw bale down on just about any level surface and plant it up. It's pretty much a portable raised bed that turns into compost at the end of the season. Straw bales are useful in situations where you have extremely poor soil (or even no soil—I've seen people garden with straw bales on their paved driveways).

If you want to try it out, get a weed-free bale. (Make sure it's straw, not hay, as the latter often contains various weed seeds.) It is necessary to condition the bale a couple of weeks before you decide to plant. You cannot just stuff plants into a fresh bale. To prepare the bale, water it every few days, alternating by adding a high-nitrogen lawn fertilizer. The bale will warm up and start to compost. Once it reaches an internal temperature of approximately 75 to 80°F (24 to 27°C), you can stop the conditioning process as it is ready to plant.

Create planting holes in the bale and fill them with potting soil. Tuck your plants inside and top up with soil. You shouldn't need to fertilize again through the season, but you will need to keep up with watering—straw bales dry out very quickly!

A couple of other things to watch for with straw bale gardening: They tend to attract ants and mice, so be prepared with deterrents. Strong odours also occasionally occur during the decomposition process.—SN

What is a potager garden? How can it work in a small space?

Potager (*puh-ta-zhay*) literally means "for the soup pot," and is synonymous for a French kitchen garden in a certain style that combines edibles with flowers and herbs in raised beds that are intensively planted. Designed with the French penchant for symmetry and sometimes formality, these gardens often feature beds organized around a central feature that are geometrically laid out with pathways and arbours. Intended to be situated right beside the kitchen, and thus viewable from the house, they are an integral part of the entire garden's design and ethos.

Potagers have their roots in medieval France of the 1500s, and were originally developed by monks and nuns to provide food and flowers for the altars.

A potager makes a ton of sense for our gardens these days. An edible, beautifully designed garden located right outside the kitchen is pleasing to the eye, accessible, and right where we can easily tend it.

Potagers are meant to be intensively planted, employing strategies such as succession planting, interplanting, and companion planting, ensuring that the gardens are productive from the beginning through to the end of the growing season. They are also biodiverse with many different species and varieties of vegetables, flowers, small fruit, and herbs.

When envisioning what your potager could be like and how it can fit into your garden's design, consider the following principles. First, think about the situation or location, such as orientation, amount of sunlight it will receive, vantage points, and how it will fit into the whole. Second, mull over the design. Potagers are almost always geometrical in nature with raised beds and pathways. The shape should be what works for you—whether it is a simple one of four beds with a central feature and perimeter with pathways of brick, gravel, or other hard surfaces separating the beds, or something more elaborate with different shapes of beds, pathway materials, and variations in the perimeter, from trellises to types of plants and more. Consider focal points and vertical use of the structures in the garden. The enclosure is important as it can be a windbreak as well as provide additional biodiversity. It also defines the garden space. Water features provide needed humidity to the surrounding air as well as sound and movement. Third, make it beautiful, with plants chosen for colour, foliage shape, textures, aromas, blooming, or harvest time. Consider too functions such as supports for other plants, and whether the plants you have chosen will be attractors of pollinators and other beneficial insects, or perhaps will repel less desirable ones. Include structures and other points of interest so the garden is beautiful in the off-season when it is dormant. The overall size is not important—it is what works for you in terms of what space you have, how much time and energy you have to cultivate and harvest it, and how you want to enjoy it.[6]—JM

This beautifully laid-out potager garden is ready for planting.

How can I set up a pallet garden?

Pallet gardening has become very popular over the years. Wood is costly, and you are upcycling something that potentially could end up in the landfill.

There are some concerns though, especially for those of us looking to plant edibles in them. Not all pallets are the same. There are a number of treatments applied to pallets. In particular, new pallets are treated to prevent the spread of pests and may display a symbol from the IPPC (International Plant Protection Convention) as to whether they have been heat treated (HT) or potentially treated with methyl bromide, which is a highly dangerous pesticide (harmful to human health as well as causing ozone depletion). Finally, some pallets, especially older ones, have travelled the world and along the way may have been exposed to noxious substances and pathogens. If the pallets you pick up do have the HT symbol, they are generally safe for edibles, with reservations.

All pallets should be cleaned before being deployed in the garden. Use a lot of soapy water and get right into all the cracks and crevices, followed by an application of horticultural-grade vinegar for further sanitizing, then allow it to dry for a while. You may want to protect the wood with an eco-friendly sealer after all that work, too.

Pallets can be used vertically, up a fence or wall, simply leaning against the surface, or tied to it, if possible. They can be made into A-frames so that there are two sides for planting, with a cord between the sides to prevent inadvertent collapse. They can be simply laid down as a single-layer bed. They can be taken apart and used to make raised beds or tabletop beds. They even make a handy shelving unit for potted plants. There are a multitude of ideas all over the web, and some are very ingenious, indeed!

The pallet gardens I have used in tight spaces worked best when I created pockets using geotextile fabric, with slings inside each of the rows. The fabric protects the wood from rotting quickly and is added insurance if there are any residual pesticides in the wood. To prevent the medium in the narrow and shallow planting areas from drying out too quickly, it may help to fill the spaces with a coir

Repurposing at its finest! Pallets can serve as an instant garden bed.

fibre-based potting soil for extra moisture retention. I also like to place the pallets out of direct afternoon sun to avoid excessive wilting.

The best plants for any configuration of a pallet garden that uses the entire pallet are those that are shallow-rooted. Flowering annuals and quick-maturing edibles such as greens, herbs, and strawberries work well. As there are limited amounts of nutrients in the medium, plan to fertilize with a liquid fertilizer regularly.

At the end of the season, take out the growing medium, thoroughly clean the pallet, and cover it for the winter to protect the wood.

In the end, the decision to use pallets, rather than purchasing wood, comes down to whether the work to prepare the pallets is worth it for you, versus buying and building your project.[7] —JM

What is an herb spiral and how is it space-saving?

Herb spirals are a vertical gardening design feature that can be hugely productive in a small space, as well as serve as a great focal point for an edible garden. They are usually a three-dimensional helix or pyramidal design, with the planting area spiralling clockwise around the centre high point. Hugely compact, twenty to thirty linear feet (six to nine metres) of planting area is compressed into a footprint roughly six feet (two metres) in diameter.

The herb spiral was the brainchild of permaculture co-founder Bill Mollison. It takes full advantage of the amount of "edge," which is often the most productive area of a garden. A very elegant structure modelled after the manifold spiral shapes found in nature, the herb spiral takes advantage of the force of gravity to distribute water around and through the structure. Because it is three-dimensional, there are multiple microclimates, with slopes, depending on which direction they face, receiving variable amounts of sunlight. The higher levels are suitable for plants that prefer drier soils, all the way down to almost moisture-heavy soils that support semi-aquatic plantings.

Herb spirals are easy to plant and to harvest from, and they have huge aesthetic value.

There are considerable temperature-moderating benefits to the design. Typically built of found materials such as stones, old bricks, blocks, and other materials that absorb heat during the day, the herb spiral then is able to release the stored heat overnight. Water is conserved both because the spiral is usually watered at the highest point, which allows it to permeate the entire structure, and since water drains in the northern hemisphere in a natural clockwise manner, water follows the curving, sloping plant area all the way to the bottom. Because the design is both compact and vertical, access to the herbs is easy, making harvesting a breeze.

To build an herb spiral, first consider where to site it. Ideally, it should be close to the kitchen as you won't want to go to the back forty of the garden to gather your herbs. It should be on level ground for safety when harvesting and not overshadowed by dense trees or neighbouring houses, as most herbs prefer full sun. Once you have the best location for your garden, lay out the area of the design, with the opening facing north. This would be where you situate your pond, if you are incorporating that feature into the spiral. A neat trick is to put a stick with string tied to it in the centre of the spiral and attach the string to a stick that you use to draw your circle. The optimum diameter is approximately six feet (two metres). Making it any larger reduces the ease of harvesting, but they can be smaller in dimension to fit your space. Next pile material in the middle to create a mound. This can be broken bricks, gravel, stones, and old branches or logs. If you use old branches, you won't need as much soil. Plus, the material makes for great drainage. Then start creating your spiral by laying bricks or stones around the outer edge, starting at the north opening. To ensure stability, dig a small trench around that edge, so the first layer is partially sunk. Then work inwards and upwards to create the spiral, ending with a small centre area at the top. Add extra garden soil, enriched with compost, to the planting area between the mounded material. Then water thoroughly and allow it to settle for a bit. This extra step gives you a chance to make sure that the structure is stable. Add extra soil if needed, for the soil profile to become established.

Populating your spiral is literally a matter of the right plant being situated in the best growing conditions for it. Herbs such as rosemary, lavender, oregano, and thyme are ideally up top in the sunniest and driest spots, followed by others that require incrementally more moisture to thrive and are oriented around the spiral according to how much sun and shade they prefer, all the way down to the moister soils where mints will flourish. Plus, if you installed a small pond to receive the

Borage is a beautiful herb with edible flowers—and it is a huge pollinator attractor as well!

extra water, water-loving species such as watercress and marsh marigolds will love being planted there. Besides culinary herbs, consider adding other plants that are more medicinal or spiritual in nature. Insectary plants that attract pollinators are also a good bet. The herb spiral is very versatile with vegetables, herbaceous perennials, and annual flowers all being great additions.[8]—JM

Vertical Gardening

4

What are the benefits of vertical gardening?
Are there any drawbacks?

Vertical gardening has become all the rage in recent years. It allows gardeners to use their creativity to place plants in spaces where they normally wouldn't be found, to add visual interest and to utilize their growing space productively. As with all things gardening, there are advantages and disadvantages to vertical gardening.

Growing up allows us to create privacy or to hide functional spaces from the rest of the garden through the use of trellises and other structures. It certainly can generate a lot of productivity for the space it uses as its footprint in the garden is small, and for those gardeners restricted to balconies, patios, or decks, it can be the difference between having a garden or not having one at all. It can also eliminate some problems, such as weed seeds blowing in and critters getting at plants (except for the black Eastern grey squirrel that is "special" to Calgary and goes anywhere, it seems). For those gardeners whose knees and backs aren't what they were, gardening on a vertical plane can be a boon. I love that I can usually be gardening my vertical gardening containers and structures early while waiting for my in-ground beds to thaw, dry out, and warm up enough for me to get in them. Plus, I get to garden standing up!

Vertical gardening comes with its own set of issues and challenges as it isn't as easy as planting into an in-ground bed. The expense of all the structures and containers can be a factor to consider, not to mention that you will need to use growing medium rather than garden soil, which comes with its own price tag. Caring for plants that are necessarily constrained from developing healthy root systems in small spaces means constant attention to watering, nutrient levels, and monitoring for pests and diseases to ensure that they are happy where they are. The range of plants is also necessarily limited to those on the smaller side and with fibrous roots rather than taproots. For me, a challenge with all my vertical gardening is at the end of the season when everything needs to be taken down, cleaned, and organized so that it is ready for next year.

There is no need to choose vertical gardening or not as your main style of gardening. In almost every garden there is room for both![1] —JM

Archways are made for vining plants such as Virginia creeper.

Classic elegance is always in style.

125

What are some suggestions to train climbing plants on walls?

Climbing plants come in three sorts, at least for gardeners on the prairies. There are tendril vines that attach to surfaces with little aerial pads that look just like mini suction cups, and, once established, do not need any support at all. The two that are common to us are Virginia creeper and its cousin Engelmann ivy. Twining vines that hold themselves up by winding their way around any handy support include grapes, hardy kiwis, clematis, honeysuckle, and bittersweet. Then there are those that are scramblers, rather than vines, and can be trained to climb or at least appear to climb. Some roses fall into this category, such as the big three Explorer roses, 'John Cabot', John Davis', and 'William Baffin', plus the massive rambler that I have along my fence, the 'Polestar'. Our prairie climate really isn't suitable for the more tender and true climbing roses that we see in other parts of the country, at least not without a lot of work each year.

Herbaceous perennial climbers such as hops or annual vines such as morning glories and sweet peas aren't suitable for training up a wall, as the effort involved would have to be repeated every year.

Tendril vines need a grid of heavy-gauge wires, both horizontal and vertical, fixed and well secured to a wall with vine eyes (special screws with a loop at the end of each screw). The horizontal wires should be twelve to eighteen inches (thirty to forty-five centimetres) apart and the vertical measurements should be about the same. The wires should not be flush to the wall, but rather about two inches (five centimetres) out.

Twining vines can be trained up a trellis or wire grid of the same dimensions. If using a trellis, ensure that the bottom doesn't quite reach the soil, so that the wood won't rot after being in contact with it for years.

When planting tendril, twining, or scrambler vines, make sure to plant them deeply and approximately eighteen inches (forty-five centimetres) out from the wall, with the root ball at a forty-five-degree angle pointing toward the supports, so that they can develop good root systems. Too close and the plants will be in the rain shadow of the wall and may suffer root damage in the winter if the soil is too warm right next to the foundation.

Attach the stems or canes to the wires or other supports with garden twine or wire encased in foam, so that they will fan out from the base. As the plants grow, continue to attach the new growth to the twine or wire until the canes have become woody and are permanently twining around the supports, or the tendril vines have enough growth to be able to adhere to the wall by themselves.

Shrubs that you wish to train up a wall require the same supports during the initial planting. They will require constant training and pruning of new growth that is projecting outwards, so that they do not revert to their shrub form, in a similar fashion to espaliering a fruit tree.[2] —JM

Will metal trellises and other supports get too hot for plants in the summer sun? Can they damage plants?

Black or dark-coloured metal trellises will absorb sunlight and heat up accordingly. Usually, however, climbing plants are affixed to a trellis by slender tendrils and stems, and the surface area that connects the plants to the trellis is small, lessening the risk of harming the plants. Think of those old wrought iron fences you see in Europe and how the plants growing against them aren't severely affected by the heat reflected off the metal. If you are worried about the potential for heat damage, try erecting a white or light-coloured trellis, or even one that is coated in plastic. Keeping the trellis out of blazing sunlight will help as well. — SN

What are some other options for vertical gardening?

You are limited only by your creativity! Consider gardens made from shoe bags, eavestroughs or plastic pipes, stepladders, stacked wooden crates, even tin cans or small pots mounted on fences and walls. We've even seen old bookcases converted into vertical gardens! Living walls are another option, of which there are countless DIY variations, or prefabricated kits you can have installed. Bear in mind that these types of set-ups may need special or extra care regarding watering, fertilizing, and other maintenance. Plant selections may be limited. It is necessary to know which type of plant fits your site and can handle being stuffed into a small space. — SN

Repurposing at its finest! Get creative with your vertical garden.

Which vining vegetables are suitable for growing vertically?

* Cucumbers
* Malabar spinach
* Pole beans: these have rounded pods, and there are many varieties, such as 'Kentucky Blue' or 'Kentucky Wonder'
* Runner beans: these have flat pods, and some varieties include 'Scarlet Emperor' and 'Painted Lady'
* Snap peas
* Snow peas
* Summer squashes: some varieties include pattypan, zucchini, and delicata
* Tomatoes
* Winter squashes: all varieties will work except the really large ones[3]—JM

Pole and runner beans are ideal candidates for vertical gardening—and they look particularly delightful on a trellis like this!

What are some great climbing plants to use as privacy screens?

Hops are an extremely fast-growing and robust perennial that can serve as an almost-instant living screen.

ANNUALS

* ✳   Black-eyed Susan (*Thunbergia alata*): twiner and flowering
* ✳   Morning glory (*Ipomoea* spp.): twiner and flowering
* ✳   Nasturtium (*Tropaeolum* spp.): edible flowers and leaves
* ✳   Sweet pea (*Lathyrus odoratus*): twiner and flowering
* ✳   Sweet potato vine (*Ipomoea batatas*): twiner and foliage

HERBACEOUS PERENNIALS

* ✳   Clematis (*Clematis* spp.): twiner (group C) and flowering
* ✳   Hops (*Humulus lupus*): twiner and fruit

* Bittersweet (*Celastrus scandens*): twiner and foliage (inedible fruit)
* Clematis (*Clematis* spp.): twiner (group A and B) and flowering
* Engelmann ivy (*Parthenocissus quinquefolia* 'Engelmannii'): tendrils and foliage
* Dropmore Scarlet honeysuckle (*Lonicera* × *brownii* 'Dropmore Scarlet'): also newer cultivars will work such as 'Mandarin' (twiner and flowering)
* Hardy kiwi (*Actinidia kolomikta* 'Arctic Beauty'): twiner and fruit-bearing

Clematis, including this gorgeous cultivar, 'Bluebird', are ideal selections for privacy screens.

* Riverbank grape (*Vitis riparia*): tendrils and fruit-bearing
* Rose (*Rosa* spp.): these flowers are not true climbers, but they can be trained to climb, especially ramblers
* Sweet autumn clematis (*Clematis terniflora*): twiner and flowering and can be rampant
* Virginia creeper (*Parthenocissus quinquefolia*): tendrils and foliage
* Wine grape (*Vitis vinifera*): twiner and fruit-bearing—JM

Have fun experimenting and exploring all the ways to grow in small spaces!
We wish you much success!

Acknowledgements

Janet and Sheryl would like to extend a massive thank you to the incredible publishing team at TouchWood Editions: Taryn Boyd (publisher), Kate Kennedy (editorial coordinator), Paula Marchese (copy editor), Tori Elliott (marketing and publicity coordinator), Tree Abraham (designer), Meg Yamamoto (proofreader), and Pat Touchie (owner).

From Janet:

What a grand journey to be on with Sheryl beside me. I literally wouldn't be on this journey without her. Long may we tread this road together!

My profound gratitude and love for all the people behind me providing love, support, and the odd boost when I need it the most. It means so much to me. Especially my family who have cooked the dinners, cleaned up around me, and even watered the garden throughout the process.

To all those gardeners, brand new and old wise ones, with your questions to challenge me and advise, tips and tricks to absorb—my grateful thanks! I love learning along with you and from you. Not a day goes by that I don't learn something in and about gardening, mostly from you all!

From Sheryl:

Janet—I know I've said it before, but you rock!

I am sending out so much love and gratitude to my family and friends—I can't thank you all enough.

Thank you to all of the gardeners and readers who have supported Janet and me since we started this book series—we couldn't (and wouldn't!) do this without you! We really hope we've helped you out on your gardening adventures so far.

Notes

Chapter One

1. Hirvela, *Edible Spots & Pots*, 2–16; Horton, "The Storied History and Enduring Life of Terra Cotta," Urban Gardens (website); Grant and Dyer, "Clay Pots vs. Plastic Pots—Should You Use Clay Pots or Plastic Pots," Gardening Know How (website); Janssen, "Choosing Clay or Plastic Pots," Institute of Agriculture and Natural Resources Nebraska Extension in Lancaster County; Sherry, "The Perfect Pot," *Fine Gardening*; Fifth Season Gardening Co. (website), "Plant Containers: Plastic vs. Fabric"; Madore, "Plastic Pots vs. Clay Pots for Plants—Pros and Cons," Green Upside (website); TerraCast Products (website), "7 Reasons Resin Planters Are Number One"; Muscato, "What Is Geotextile Fabric?—Definition & Types," Study.com (website); Matos, "Fabric Pots vs. Plastic Pots: Which Is Better?," Geopot (website).

2. Markham et al., "Effect of Container Color on Substrate Temperatures and Growth of Red Maple and Redbud," American Society for Horticultural Science.

3. Daughtry and Gaster, "Rocks in Pots: Drainage or Perched Water Table Problems?," North Carolina Cooperative Extension.

4. Hirvela, *Edible Spots & Pots*, 29–35; University of Illinois Extension, "Using Soil and Soil Mixes"; Sweetser, "How to Make Your Own Potting Soil: A DIY Potting Mix Recipe for Container Gardening," *The Old Farmer's Almanac*; University of Saskatchewan College of Agriculture and Bioresources, "What Kind of Soil Should I Use in My Containers?"; University of Maryland Extension, "'Soil' for Containers: Choose a Good Growing Medium for Container Gardens"; Iannotti, "Soilless Potting Mix," The Spruce (website); Buechel, "Simplifying Organic Growing: The Best Growing Media Components," Pro-Mix (website); Lopez, "What Are the Grades of Peat Moss?," Pro-Mix (website).

5. University of Illinois Extension, "Using Soil and Soil Mixes"; Spring Pot (website), "Gardener's Guide to Reuse Potting Soil"; Pleasant, "Nifty, Thrifty Ways to Reuse Potting Soil," GrowVeg (website).

6. Matos, "Fabric Pots vs. Plastic Pots: Which Is Better?," Geopot (website).

7. Gardener's Supply Company (website), "Using the Potato Grow Bag"; B. Grant, "Container Potatoes—How to Grow Potatoes in a Container," Gardening Know How (website).

8. G. Buster and M. Buster "Global Buckets: Two Buckets on a Mission to Reduce Malnutrition," Global Buckets (website).

9. Rindels, "Cleaning and Disinfecting Plant Containers," Iowa State University Extension and Outreach; Dengarden (website), "Recycling and Reusing Seedling Trays and Pots in the Backyard Garden"; Rose, "How to Clean Garden Pots," Garden Therapy (website).

10. Hirvela, *Edible Spots & Pots*, 18; Downey, "What to Put in the Bottom of a Large Planter," SFGate (website); Michaels, "5 Tips for Beautiful Large Container Gardens," The Spruce (website); Levins, "3 Myths about Gardening with Styrofoam Debunked," Air Sea Containers (website).

11. Michaels, "10 Tips for Watering Plants Growing in Containers," The Spruce (website); Gardener's Supply Company (website), "How to Water Raised Beds"; Smith, "A Guide to Watering Your Container Garden," Guardian.

12. American Museum of Natural History (website), "Superabsorbent Hydrogels: A Study of the Most Effective Application of Cross-linked Polyacrylamide Polymers."

13. Dyer, "What Are Hydrogels: Learn about Water Crystals in Potting Soil," Gardening Know How (website); Grist (website), "Are Plastic Soil Beads Safe for My Plants?"; Chalker-Scott, "The Myth of Polyacrylamide Hydrogels: Polyacrylamide Hydrogels Are Environmentally Safe Substances That Reduce Irrigation Needs," Washington State University (PDF); Royal Horticultural Society (website), "Water-Retaining Granules"; Schalau, "Hydrogels: Are They Safe?," University of Arizona Cooperative Extension.

14. Age Old Organics (website), "Remember to Flush: Removing Excessive Salt Build-Up"; Coe, "How to Use Vinegar and Water to Flush Salt Build Up Out of Soil," Garden Guides (website); Filipski, "Reduce Salt to Keep Plants Crust-Free and Healthy," Edmonton Journal.

15. Dabbs, "Creating Beautiful Hanging Baskets," Post and Courier; Fortune, "How to Plant Stunning Hanging Baskets and Containers," Chatelaine; Woodard, "Hanging Flower Baskets: 5 Secrets the Pros Use," The Garden Glove (website).

16. Ipatenco, "How to Keep Hanging Flower Baskets Looking Fresh," SFGate (website); Old World Garden Farms (website), "How to Rejuvenate Worn Out Hanging Baskets and Potted Plants"; Pearce, "Top Tips for Keeping Hanging Baskets Looking Great!," Garden Works (website).

17. Hole and Woods, Herbs & Edible Flowers, 22; Small and Deutsch, Culinary Herbs for Short-Season Gardeners, 170–73; Burpee (website), "How to Bring Tender Herbs Inside for Winter"; Vanderlinden, "How to Overwinter Garden Herbs Indoors," The Spruce (website).

18. University of Saskatchewan College of Agriculture and Bioresources, "Didn't Quite Get It All Planted? Overwintering Hardy Potted Plants"; Parsons, "Wintering Trees and Shrubs Grown in Containers," Manitoba Co-operator (website); Fosdick, "Over-Wintering Your Perennials in Pots? Some Tips," Associated Press.

19. Corkery, "You Can Overwinter Tulips in Pots," Chicago Tribune; Cullen, "Spring-Flowering Bulbs in Containers," MarkCullen.com (website); Hartlage, "Planting Spring Bulbs in Containers," Fine Gardening; Old House Gardens (website), "Growing Bulbs in Pots."

20. Burnett, "Fungus Gnats: How to Identify and Get Rid of Fungus Gnats," The Old Farmer's Almanac; Missouri Botanical Garden (website), "Fungus Gnats"; How Stuff Works (website), "How to Kill Fungus Gnats"; Sproule, "Fungus Gnats," Salisbury Greenhouse (website); Gifford, "How to Control Fungus Gnats and Damping Off Organically," Small Footprint Family (website); Andrychowicz, "Fungus Gnats vs. Fruit Flies: What's the Difference?," Get Busy Gardening (website).

21. Toronto Master Gardeners (website), "Pollinator Garden: A Toronto Master Gardener's Guide."

22. Michaels, "10 Best Vegetables That Grow in Containers," The Spruce (website); Balcony Garden Web (website), "Best Vegetables to Grow in Pots: Most Productive Vegetables for Containers"; Sweetser, "Container Growing with Vegetables: Container Gardening Yields More Vegetables with Less Work!," *The Old Farmer's Almanac*; Walliser, "Container Vegetable Plants: The Best Varieties for Success," Savvy Gardening (website); Macdonald, "Growing Food in Containers," West Coast Seeds (website).

23. Michaels, "9 Great Foliage Plants for Container Gardens," The Spruce (website); Tornio, "Top 10 Container Foliage Plants," Birds and Blooms (website).

Chapter Two

1. American Galvanizers Association (website), "In Contact with Food."

2. Government of Canada, "Staying Safe around Treated Wood."

3. Eakes, "A New Generation of Pressure-Treated Wood," *Home Builder*.

4. Binzen, "Food-Safe Finishes," *Fine Woodworking*; James, "Is Linseed Oil Toxic?," Gimme the Good Stuff (website).

5. Madore, "Should You Line a Raised Garden Bed? (Read This First)," Green Upside (website).

6. Avis, "From the Bottom Up—A DIY Guide to Wicking Beds," Verge Permaculture (website); Deep Green Permaculture (website), "Wicking Bed Construction, How to Build a Self-Watering Wicking Bed."

7. *The Old Farmer's Almanac*, "How to Build a Raised Garden Bed: Planning, Building, and Planting a Raised Garden Bed"; Nolan, "The Best Soil for a Raised Garden Bed," Savvy Gardening (website).

8. Bartholomew, *All New Square Foot Gardening*, 40–46, 86–100, 108–12, 137–40; Nick, "The Pros and Cons of Square Foot Gardening," *Good Housekeeping*; Dore, "Planning a Square Foot Vegetable Garden," GrowVeg (website).

9. Hemenway, *Gaia's Garden*, 85–90; Lanza, "Lasagna Gardening," *Mother Earth News*; de Jauregui, "The Disadvantages of Lasagna Gardening," SFGate (website); Blackwell, "Make a Lasagna Garden in a Raised Bed," Brooklyn Botanic Garden (website); A. Grant and B. Grant, "Lasagna Gardening Pros and Cons," Gardening Know How (website).

10. Hemenway, *Gaia's Garden*, 85; Miles, "The Art and Science of Making a Hügelkultur Bed—Transforming Woody Debris into a Garden Resource," Permaculture Research Institute (website); *Inspiration Green and Permaculture*, "The Many Benefits of Hügelkultur."

Chapter Three

1. Rhoades, "Tips on Making Microclimates—How to Make a Microclimate," Gardening Know How (website); Vanheems, "Plan Your Garden to Create Perfect Microclimates," GrowVeg (website); BC Farms & Food, "Creating Microclimates to Protect Plants"; A. Miller, "Creating Your Own Micro-Climate," *Mother Earth News*.

2. Iannotti, "What Does Crafting Mean?," The Spruce (website).

3. Massingham Hart, *Vertical Vegetables & Fruit*, 138–41; Chicago Botanic Garden (website), "Espalier an Apple Tree"; Pokorny, "Training a Fruit Tree into an Espalier Takes a Good Dash of Dedication," Oregon State University Extension Service; Rose, "The Art of Espalier: Growing Fruit Trees in Small Spaces," Garden Therapy (website).

4. City of Calgary, "YardSmart—Trees and Shrubs"; Calgary Plants Online Garden Centre (website), "Trees—Columnar or Narrow"; Dobson, "Plant This, Not That: If You Want Cedar, Plant Upright Juniper," *Calgary Herald*; Sunstar Nurseries (website), "Evergreens"; Mendonca, "Top Columnar Trees to Plant in Alberta," Sherwood Nurseries (website); Sunstar Nurseries (website), "Deciduous Trees"; University of Saskatchewan Fruit Program, "Sour Cherries."

5. Fowler, "Intercropping and Catch Cropping," Seed Parade (website); Beaulieu, "Nitrogen-Fixing Plants That Aid in Fertilization," The Spruce (website); Wagner, "Biological Nitrogen Fixation," The Nature Education Knowledge Project.

6. Oder, "How to Design a Potager Garden," Treehugger (website); Brennan, *In the French Kitchen Garden*, 9–35; Jabbour, *Groundbreaking Food Gardens*, 34–36; Hendry, "How to Design a Potager Garden," GrowVeg (website).

7. Spencer, "Is Pallet Gardening Safe?," The Micro Farm Project (website); Universal Pallets (website), "Ultimate Guide to Pallet Markings"; Pennington, "The One Thing You Need to Know If You're Considering a Pallet Garden," The Kitchn (website); Travis, "Making a Basic Pallet Garden," Sunday Gardener (website).

8. Hemenway, *Gaia's Garden*, 39–40; Mars, *The Basics of Permaculture Design*, 11; Gibson, "15 Benefits of a Herb Spiral in Your Garden," The Micro Gardener (website); Gibson, "4 Step Guide to Building a Herb Spiral," The Micro Gardener (website); Engels, "The Magic and Mystery of Constructing a Herb Spiral and Why Every Suburban Lawn Should Have One," Permaculture Research Institute (website).

Chapter Four

1. Dyer and Ellis, "Vertical Gardening Pros and Cons," Gardening Know How (website); M. Miller, "The Pros and Cons of a Vertical Garden," Natural News (website); Garden Tabs (website), "Vertical Gardening Pros and Cons."

2. Royal Horticultural Society (website), "Climbers: Training and Pruning on Planting"; *BBC Gardeners' World*, "Tips for Training Climbing Plants"; Hodgson, "Do Climbing Plants Damage Walls?," Laidback Gardener (website); Spengler, "Best Plants to Cover Walls—Tips for Using Plants on Walls," Gardening Know How (website); Hofer, "Types of Climbing Vines," *Fine Gardening*.

3. Jones, "12 Climbing Vegetables That Will Thrive When Trained Up Garden Walls," Garden & Happy (website).

Sources

Age Old Organics (website). "Remember to Flush: Removing Excessive Salt Build-Up." Accessed May 8, 2020. ageold.com/remember-to-flush-removing-excessive-salt -build-up/.

American Galvanizers Association (website). "In Contact with Food." Accessed May 9, 2020. galvanizeit.org/hot-dip-galvanizing/how-long-does-hdg-last/contact-with-food.

American Museum of Natural History (website). "Superabsorbent Hydrogels: A Study of the Most Effective Application of Cross-linked Polyacrylamide Polymers." 2009. amnh.org/learn-teach/curriculum-collections/young-naturalist-awards/winning -essays/2009/superabsorbant-hydrogels-a-study-of-the-most-effective-application-of-cross -linked-polyacrylamide-polymers.

Andrychowicz, Amy. "Fungus Gnats vs. Fruit Flies: What's the Difference?" Get Busy Gardening (website). Accessed May 8, 2020. getbusygardening.com/fungus-gnats-vs -fruit-flies/.

Avis, Rob. "From the Bottom Up—A DIY Guide to Wicking Beds." Verge Permaculture (website). May 30, 2011. vergepermaculture.ca/2011/05/30/guide-to-wicking-beds/.

Balcony Garden Web (website). "Best Vegetables to Grow in Pots: Most Productive Vegetables for Containers." Accessed May 9, 2020. balconygardenweb.com/best -vegetables-to-grow-in-pots-most-productive-vegetables/.

Bartholomew, Mel. *All New Square Foot Gardening.* 3rd ed. Beverly, MA: Cool Springs Press, 2018.

BBC *Gardeners' World.* "Tips for Training Climbing Plants." May 19, 2019. gardenersworld.com/plants/tips-for-training-climbing-plants/.

BC Farms & Food (website). "Creating Microclimates to Protect Plants." June 27, 2016. bcfarmsandfood.com/creating-microclimates-to-protect-plants/.

Beaulieu, David. "Nitrogen-Fixing Plants That Aid in Fertilization." The Spruce (website). October 18, 2019. thespruce.com/nitrogen-fixing-plants-2131092.

Binzen, Jonathan. "Food-Safe Finishes." *Fine Woodworking.* March/April 1998. finewoodworking.com/2006/08/01/food-safe-finishes.

Blackwell, Jenny. "Make a Lasagna Garden in a Raised Bed." Brooklyn Botanic Garden (website). September 23, 2016. bbg.org/gardening/article/make_a_lasagna_garden _in_a_raised_bed.

Brennan, Georgeanne. *In the French Kitchen Garden: The Joys of Cultivating a Potager.* San Francisco: Chronicle Books, 1998.

Buechel, Troy. "Simplifying Organic Growing: The Best Growing Media Components." Pro-Mix (website). October 5, 2018. pthorticulture.com/en/training -center/simplifying-organic-growing-the-best-growing-media-components/.

Burnett, Christopher. "Fungus Gnats: How to Identify and Get Rid of Fungus Gnats." *The Old Farmer's Almanac.* Accessed May 8, 2020. almanac.com/pest/fungus-gnats.

Burpee (website). "How to Bring Tender Herbs Inside for Winter." Accessed May 8, 2020. burpee.com/gardenadvicecenter/herbs/general-gardening/how-to-bring-tender -herbs-inside-for-winter/article10786.html#.

Buster, Grant, and Max Buster. "Global Buckets: Two Buckets on a Mission to Reduce Malnutrition." Global Buckets (website). globalbuckets.org.

Calgary Plants Online Garden Centre (website). "Trees—Columnar or Narrow." Accessed May 4, 2020. calgaryplants.com/collections/tress-that-are-columnar-or-narrow.

Chalker-Scott, Linda. "The Myth of Polyacrylamide Hydrogels: Polyacrylamide Hydrogels Are Environmentally Safe Substances That Reduce Irrigation Needs." Washington State University (PDF). Accessed May 8, 2020. s3.wp.wsu.edu/uploads /sites/403/2015/03/hydrogels.pdf.

Chicago Botanic Garden (website). "Espalier an Apple Tree." Accessed May 4, 2020. chicagobotanic.org/plantinfo/espalier_apple_tree.

City of Calgary. "YardSmart—Trees and Shrubs." Accessed May 4, 2020. calgary.ca /UEP/Water/Pages/Water-conservation/Lawn-and-garden/Water-wise-gardening-and -plants/Water-Wise-Trees-and-Shrubs.aspx.

Coe, Robin. "How to Use Vinegar and Water to Flush Salt Build Up Out of Soil." Garden Guides (website). September 21, 2017. gardenguides.com/94545-use-vinegar -water-flush-salt-build-up-out-soil.html.

Corkery, Denise. "You Can Overwinter Tulips in Pots. Chicago Tribune. September 21 2008. chicagotribune.com/news/ct-xpm-2008-09-21-0809180445-story.html.

Cullen, Mark. "Spring-Flowering Bulbs in Containers." MarkCullen.com (website). November 30, 2011. markcullen.com/spring-flowering-bulbs-in-containers/.

Dabbs, Amy. "Creating Beautiful Hanging Baskets." Post and Courier. June 5, 2015. postandcourier.com/features/home_and_garden/creating-beautiful-hanging-baskets /article_07697be3-9510-51b4-9e6d-1577d8cb8d64.html.

Daughtry, Minda, and Rhonda Gaster. "Rocks in Pots: Drainage or Perched Water Table Problems?" North Carolina Cooperative Extension. December 4, 2018. lee.ces .ncsu.edu/2018/12/rocks-in-pots-drainage-or-perched-water-table-problems/.

Deep Green Permaculture (website). "Wicking Bed Construction, How to Build a Self-Watering Wicking Bed." Accessed May 9, 2020. deepgreenpermaculture.com/diy -instructions/wicking-bed-construction/.

de Jauregui, Ruth. "The Disadvantages of Lasagna Gardening." SFGate (website). Last updated June 12, 2020. homeguides.sfgate.com/disadvantages-lasagna-gardening-71023 .html.

Dengarden (website). "Recycling and Reusing Seedling Trays and Pots in the Backyard Garden." May 8, 2019. dengarden.com/gardening/Recycling-and-Reusing-Seedling -Trays-and-Pots-in-the-Backyard-Garden.

Dobson, Carole. "Plant This, Not That: If You Want Cedar, Plant Upright Juniper." Calgary Herald. May 17, 2012. calgaryherald.com/life/plant+this+that+want+cedar +plant+upright+juniper/6640292/story.html.

Dore, Jeremy. "Planning a Square Foot Vegetable Garden." GrowVeg (website). July 30, 2010. growveg.com/guides/planning-a-square-foot-vegetable-garden/.

Downey, Lillian. "What to Put in the Bottom of a Large Planter." SFGate (website). Last updated December 17, 2018. homeguides.sfgate.com/put-bottom-large-planter -37465.html.

Dyer, Mary H. "What Are Hydrogels: Learn about Water Crystals in Potting Soil." Gardening Know How (website). Last updated April 4, 2018. gardeningknowhow.com /special/containers/water-crystals-in-potting-soil.htm.

Dyer, Mary H., and Mary Ellen Ellis. "Vertical Gardening Pros and Cons." Gardening Know How (website). July 10, 2018. blog.gardeningknowhow.com/gardening-pros-cons /vertical-gardening-pros-and-cons-2/.

Eakes, Jon. "A New Generation of Pressure-Treated Wood." Home Builder. Accessed May 12, 2020. homebuildercanada.com/2602_deck.htm.

Engels, Jonathon. "The Magic and Mystery of Constructing a Herb Spiral and Why Every Suburban Lawn Should Have One." Permaculture Research Institute (website). April 17, 2015. permaculturenews.org/2015/04/17/the-magic-and-mystery-of -constructing-an-herb-spiral-and-why-every-suburban-lawn-should-have-one/.

Fifth Season Gardening Co. (website). "Plant Containers: Plastic vs. Fabric." September 29, 2015. fifthseasongardening.com/plant-containers-plastic-vs-fabric.

Filipski, Gerald. "Reduce Salt to Keep Plants Crust-Free and Healthy." Edmonton Journal. February 27, 2015. edmontonjournal.com/reduce+salt+keep+plants+crust+free +healthy/10848607/story.html#:~:text=Using%20rainwater%20or%20melted%20snow ,added%20to%20the%20tap%20water.

Fortune, Nancy. "How to Plant Stunning Hanging Baskets and Containers." Chatelaine. Last updated May 9, 2018. chatelaine.com/home-decor/how-to-plant -stunning-hanging-baskets-and-containers/.

Fosdick, Dean. "Over-Wintering Your Perennials in Pots? Some Tips." Associated Press. October 7, 2014. globalnews.ca/news/1602975/over-wintering-your-perennials-in-pots -some-tips/.

Fowler, Helen. "Intercropping and Catch Cropping." Seed Parade (website). May 16, 2013. seedparade.co.uk/news/sowing/intercropping-and-catch-cropping/.

Gardener's Supply Company (website). "How to Water Raised Beds." Last updated February 12, 2019. gardeners.com/how-to/raised-bed-watering/8962.html.

———. "Using the Potato Grow Bag." Last updated April 26, 2020. gardeners.com /how-to/potato-grow-bag-instructions/7099.html.

Garden Tabs (website). "Vertical Gardening Pros and Cons." Accessed May 2, 2020. gardentabs.com/pros-cons/.

Gibson, Anne. "15 Benefits of a Herb Spiral in Your Garden." The Micro Gardener (website). Accessed May 9, 2020. themicrogardener.com/15-benefits-of-a-herb-spiral-in -your-garden/

———. "4 Step Guide to Building a Herb Spiral." The Micro Gardener (website). Accessed May 9, 2020. themicrogardener.com/4-step-guide-to-building-a-herb-spiral/.

Gifford, Dawn. "How to Control Fungus Gnats and Damping Off Organically." Small Footprint Family (website) Accessed May 8, 2020. smallfootprintfamily.com/how-to -control-fungus-gnats-organically.

Government of Canada. "Staying Safe around Treated Wood." Last modified January 14, 2019. canada.ca/en/health-canada/services/consumer-product-safety/reports -publications/pesticides-pest-management/fact-sheets-other-resources/staying-safe -around-treated-wood.html.

Grant, Amy, and Bonnie Grant. "Lasagna Gardening Pros and Cons." Gardening Know How (website). September 11, 2018. blog.gardeningknowhow.com/gardening-pros-cons /lasagna-gardening-pros-and-cons-2/.

Grant, Bonnie, and Mary H. Dyer. "Clay Pots vs. Plastic Pots—Should You Use Clay Pots or Plastic Pots." Gardening Know How (website). January 7, 2020. blog .gardeningknowhow.com/gardening-pros-cons/clay-pots-vs-plastic-pots/.

Grant, Bonnie L. "Container Potatoes—How to Grow Potatoes in a Container." Gardening Know How (website). Last updated April 28, 2020. gardeningknowhow.com /edible/vegetables/potato/container-potatoes.htm.

Grist (website). "Are Plastic Soil Beads Safe for My Plants?" April 18, 2016. grist.org /living/are-plastic-soil-beads-safe-for-my-plants/.

Hartlage, Richard. "Planting Spring Bulbs in Containers." Fine Gardening, issue 78 Accessed May 9, 2020. finegardening.com/article/planting-spring-bulbs-in-containers.

Hemenway, Toby. Gaia's Garden: A Guide to Home-Scale Permaculture. 2nd ed. White River Junction, VT: Chelsea Green Publishing, 2009.

Hendry, Ann Marie. "How to Design a Potager Garden." GrowVeg (website). December 30, 2011. growveg.com/guides/how-to-design-a-potager-garden/.

Hinvela, Stacey. Edible Spots & Pots: Small-Space Gardens for Growing Vegetables and Herbs in Containers, Raised Beds, and More. Emmaus, PA: Rodale, 2014.

Hodgson, Larry. "Do Climbing Plants Damage Walls?" Laidback Gardener (website). September 24, 2018. laidbackgardener.blog/tag/do-climbing-plants-damage-walls/.

Hofer, Marie. "Types of Climbing Vines." Fine Gardening. Accessed May 2, 2020. finegardening.com/article/types-of-climbing-vines.

Hole, Lois, and Earl J. Woods. Herbs & Edible Flowers: Gardening for the Kitchen. St. Albert, AB: Hole's, 2000.

Horton, Robin Plaskoff. "The Storied History and Enduring Life of Terra Cotta." Urban Gardens (website) February 26, 2018. urbangardensweb.com/2018/02/26/storied -history-enduring-life-terra-cotta/.

How Stuff Works (website). "How to Kill Fungus Gnats." Accessed May 8, 2020. home .howstuffworks.com/how-to-kill-fungus-gnats.htm.

Iannotti, Marie. "Soilless Potting Mix." The Spruce (website). Last updated October 28, 2019. thespruce.com/what-is-a-soilless-potting-mix-1403085.

———. "What Does Grafting Mean?" The Spruce (website). Last updated October 21, 2019. thespruce.com/what-does-grafting-mean-4125565.

Inspiration Green and Permaculture. "The Many Benefits of Hügelkultur." October 17, 2013. permaculture.co.uk/articles/many-benefits-hügelkultur.

Ipatenco, Sara. "How to Keep Hanging Flower Baskets Looking Fresh." SFGate (website). Accessed May 8, 2020. homeguides.sfgate.com/keep-hanging-flower-baskets -looking-fresh-21914.html.

Jabbour, Niki. *Groundbreaking Food Gardens: 73 Plans That Will Change the Way You Grow Your Garden*. North Adams, MA: Storey Publishing, 2014.

James, Maia. "Is Linseed Oil Toxic?" Gimme the Good Stuff (website). February 1, 2016. gimmethegoodstuff.org/is-linseed-oil-toxic/.

Janssen, Don. "Choosing Clay or Plastic Pots." Institute of Agriculture and Natural Resources Nebraska Extension in Lancaster County. Last updated March 2008. lancaster.unl.edu/hort/articles/2002/typeofpots.shtml.

Jones, Elizabeth. "12 Climbing Vegetables That Will Thrive When Trained Up Garden Walls." Garden & Happy (website). Accessed May 2, 2020. gardenandhappy .com/climbing-vegetables/.

Lanza, Patricia. "Lasagna Gardening." *Mother Earth News*. April/May 1999. motherearthnews.com/organic-gardening/lasagna-gardening-zmaz99amztak.

Levins, Cory. "3 Myths about Gardening with Styrofoam Debunked." Air Sea Containers (website). May 16, 2018. airseacontainers.com/blog/3-myths-about -gardening-with-styrofoam-debunked/.

Lopez, Jose Chen. "What Are the Grades of Peat Moss?" Pro-Mix (website). March 30, 2020. pthorticulture.com/en/training-center/what-are-the-grades-of-peat-moss/.

Macdonald, Mark. "Growing Food in Containers." West Coast Seeds (website). March 5, 2020. westcoastseeds.com/blogs/garden-wisdom/growing-food-containers.

Madore, Jonathon David. "Plastic Pots vs. Clay Pots for Plants—Pros and Cons." Green Upside (website). Accessed July 14, 2020. greenupside.com/plastic-pots-vs-clay-pots-for -plants-pros-and-cons/.

———. "Should You Line a Raised Garden Bed? (Read This First)." Green Upside (website). Accessed May 9, 2020. greenupside.com/should-you-line-a-raised-garden-bed -plus-what-to-use/.

Markham, John W., III, Dale J. Bremer, Cheryl R. Boyer, and Kenneth R. Schroeder. "Effect of Container Color on Substrate Temperatures and Growth of Red Maple and Redbud." American Society for Horticultural Science. May 2011. journals.ashs.org /hortsci/view/journals/hortsci/46/5/article-p721.xml.

Mars, Ross. *The Basics of Permaculture Design*. White River Junction, VT: Chelsea Green Publishing, 2005.

Massingham Hart, Rhonda. *Vertical Vegetables & Fruit: Creative Gardening Techniques for Growing Up in Small Spaces*. North Adams, MA: Storey Publishing, 2011.

Matos, Sean. "Fabric Pots vs. Plastic Pots: Which Is Better?" Geopot (website). March 1, 2018. geopot.com/blogs/about-fabric-pots/fabric-pots-vs-plastic-pots.

Mendonca, Sarah. "Top Columnar Trees to Plant in Alberta." Sherwood Nurseries (website). July 4, 2019. sherwoodnurseries.ca/top-columnar-trees-to-plant-in-alberta/.

Michaels, Kerry. "5 Tips for Beautiful Large Container Gardens." The Spruce (website). Last updated on July 15, 2019. thespruce.com/tips-for-planting-large -container-gardens-848022.

————. "9 Great Foliage Plants for Container Gardens." The Spruce (website). Last updated November 5, 2019. thespruce.com/foliage-plants-for-container -gardens-848029.

————. "10 Best Vegetables That Grow in Containers." The Spruce (website). Last updated April 20, 2020. thespruce.com/great-vegetables-to-grow-in-containers-848214.

————. "10 Tips for Watering Plants Growing in Containers." The Spruce (website). Last updated January 29, 2019. thespruce.com/watering-plants-in-containers-847785.

Miles, Melissa. "The Art and Science of Making a Hügelkultur Bed—Transforming Woody Debris into a Garden Resource." Permaculture Research Institute (website). August 3, 2010. permaculturenews.org/2010/08/03/the-art-and-science-of-making-a -hugelkultur-bed-transforming-woody-debris-into-a-garden-resource/.

Miller, Aaron. "Creating Your Own Micro-Climate." *Mother Earth News*. March 11, 2014. motherearthnews.com/organic-gardening/creating-your-own-micro-climate -zbcz1403.

Miller, Mary. "The Pros and Cons of a Vertical Garden." Natural News (website). December 11, 2018. naturalnews.com/2018-12-11-the-pros-and-cons-of-a-vertical -garden.html.

Missouri Botanical Garden (website). "Fungus Gnats." Accessed May 8, 2020. missouribotanicalgarden.org/gardens-gardening/your-garden/help-for-the-home -gardener/advice-tips-resources/pests-and-problems/insects/flies/fungus gnats.aspx.

Muscato, Christopher. "What Is Geotextile Fabric?—Definition & Types." Study.com (website). Accessed May 7, 2020. study.com/academy/lesson/what-is-geotextile-fabric -definition-types.html.

Nick, Jean. "The Pros and Cons of Square Foot Gardening." *Good Housekeeping*. July 30, 2018. goodhousekeeping.com/home/gardening/a20706747/square-foot-gardening/.

Nolan, Tara. "The Best Soil for a Raised Garden Bed." Savvy Gardening (website). savvygardening.com/the-best-soil-for-a-raised-garden-bed/.

Oder, Tom. "How to Design a Potager Garden." Treehugger (website). May 31, 2017. treehugger.com/how-design-potager-garden-4863948.

The Old Farmer's Almanac. "How to Build a Raised Garden Bed: Planning, Building, and Planting a Raised Garden Bed." January 10, 2020. almanac.com/content/how -build-raised-garden-bed.

Old House Gardens (website). "Growing Bulbs in Pots." Accessed May 9, 2020. oldhousegardens.com/BulbsInPots.

Old World Garden Farms (website). "How to Rejuvenate Worn Out Hanging Baskets and Potted Plants." July 21, 2016. oldworldgardenfarms.com/2016/07/21/rejuvenating -hanging-baskets/.

Parsons, Albert. "Wintering Trees and Shrubs Grown in Containers." Manitoba Co-operator (website). October 26, 2018. manitobacooperator.ca/country-crossroads /wintering-trees-and-shrubs-grown-in-containers/.

Pearce, Scott. "Top Tips for Keeping Hanging Baskets Looking Great!" Garden Works (website). Accessed May 8, 2020. gardenworks.ca/2017/05/10/top-tips-keeping-hanging -baskets-looking-great/.

Pennington, Amy. "The One Thing You Need to Know If You're Considering a Pallet Garden." The Kitchn (website). June 5, 2017. thekitchn.com/what-you-should-know -about-pallet-gardening-244725.

Pleasant, Barbara. "Nifty, Thrifty Ways to Reuse Potting Soil." GrowVeg (website). September 27, 2018. growveg.com/guides/nifty-thrifty-ways-to-reuse-potting-soil/.

Pokorny, Kym. "Training a Fruit Tree into an Espalier Takes a Good Dash of Dedication." Oregon State University Extension Service. July 2015. extension .oregonstate.edu/news/training-fruit-tree-espalier-takes-good-dash-dedication.

Rhoades, Jackie. "Tips on Making Microclimates—How to Make a Microclimate." Gardening Know How (website). Last updated April 5, 2018. gardeningknowhow.com /garden-how-to/projects/how-to-make-a-microclimate.htm.

Rindels, Sherry. "Cleaning and Disinfecting Plant Containers." Iowa State University Extension and Outreach. March 16, 1994. hortnews.extension.iastate.edu/1994/3-16 -1994/clean.html.

Rose, Stephanie. "The Art of Espalier: Growing Fruit Trees in Small Spaces." Garden Therapy (website). March 11, 2018. gardentherapy.ca/espalier-fruit-trees/.

———. "How to Clean Garden Pots." Garden Therapy (website). April 18, 2018. gardentherapy.ca/how-to-clean-garden-pots/.

Royal Horticultural Society (website). "Climbers: Training and Pruning on Planting." Accessed May 2, 2020. rhs.org.uk/advice/profile?PID=463.

———. "Water-Retaining Granules." Accessed May 8, 2020. rhs.org.uk/advice /profile?PID=692

Schalau, Jeff. "Hydrogels: Are They Safe?" University of Arizona Cooperative Extension. January 14, 2009. cals.arizona.edu/yavapai/anr/hort/byg/archive/hydrogels .html.

Sherry, Danielle. "The Perfect Pot." Fine Gardening, issue 118. Accessed May 7, 2020. finegardening.com/article/the-perfect-pot.

Small, Ernest, and Grace Deutsch. Culinary Herbs for Short-Season Gardeners. Ottawa: National Research Council of Canada Research Press, 2001.

Smith, Mark Ridsdill. "A Guide to Watering Your Container Garden." Guardian. July 18, 2014. theguardian.com/lifeandstyle/2014/jul/18/guide-watering-container-garden.

Spencer, Kari. "Is Pallet Gardening Safe?" The Micro Farm Project (website). February 25, 2015. themicrofarmproject.com/blog/is-pallet-gardening-safe.

Spengler, Teo. "Best Plants to Cover Walls—Tips for Using Plants on Walls." Gardening Know How (website). gardeningknowhow.com/garden-how-to/design/lideas/using-plants-on-walls.htm.

Spring Pot (website). "Gardener's Guide to Reuse Potting Soil." March 22, 2017. springpot.com/reusing-potting-soil/.

Sproule, Rob. "Fungus Gnats." Salisbury Greenhouse (website). Accessed May 8, 2020. salisburygreenhouse.com/fungus-gnats/.

Sunstar Nurseries (website). "Deciduous Trees." Accessed May 4, 2020. sunstarnurseries.com/deciduous-trees.html.

———. "Evergreens." Accessed May 4, 2020. sunstarnurseries.com/evergreens.html.

Sweetser, Robin. "Container Growing with Vegetables: Container Gardening Yields More Vegetables with Less Work!" *The Old Farmer's Almanac*. January 22, 2020. almanac.com/content/container-gardening-vegetables.

———. "How to Make Your Own Potting Soil: A DIY Potting Mix Recipe for Container Gardening." *The Old Farmer's Almanac*. January 22, 2020. almanac.com/news/gardening-news/make-your-own-potting-soil.

TerraCast Products (website). "7 Reasons Resin Planters Are Number One." November 27, 2014. terracastproducts.com/7-reasons-resin-planters-number-one/.

Tornio, Stacy. "Top 10 Container Foliage Plants." Birds and Blooms (website). Accessed May 9, 2020. birdsandblooms.com/gardening/small-space-gardening/top-10-container-foliage-favorites/.

Toronto Master Gardeners (website). "Pollinator Garden: A Toronto Master Gardener's Guide." Last updated February 2015. torontomastergardeners.ca/gardeningguides/pollinator-garden-a-toronto-master-gardeners-guide/.

Travis, Karen. "Making a Basic Pallet Garden." Sunday Gardener (website). Last updated September 30, 2019. sundaygardener.net/making-a-basic-pallet-garden/.

Universal Pallets (website). "Ultimate Guide to Pallet Markings." January 2018. universalpallets.com/2018/01/ultimate-guide-pallet-markings/.

University of Illinois Extension. "Using Soil and Soil Mixes." Accessed May 7, 2020. web.extension.illinois.edu/containergardening/soil.cfm.

University of Maryland Extension. "'Soil' for Containers: Choose a Good Growing Medium for Container Gardens." Accessed May 7, 2020. extension.umd.edu/hgic/topics/soil-containers.

University of Saskatchewan College of Agriculture and Bioresources. "Didn't Quite Get It All Planted? Overwintering Hardy Potted Plants." February 7, 2018. gardening.usask.ca/articles-how-to/didnt-quite-get-it all-planted-overwintering-hardy-potted-plants.php.

———. "What Kind of Soil Should I Use in My Containers?" February 7, 2018. gardening.usask.ca/article-list-soils/what-kind-of-soil-should-i-use-in-my-containers.php.

University of Saskatchewan Fruit Program. "Sour Cherries." Accessed May 4, 2020. research-groups.usask.ca/fruit/Fruit%20crops/sour-cherries.php.

Vanderlinden, Colleen. "How to Overwinter Garden Herbs Indoors." The Spruce (website). Last updated September 30, 2019. thespruce.com/growing-garden-herbs -indoors-during-winter-2540050.

Vanheems, Benedict. "Plan Your Garden to Create Perfect Microclimates." GrowVeg (website). February 8, 2018. growveg.com/guides/plan-your-garden-to-create-perfect -microclimates/.

Wagner, Stephen C. "Biological Nitrogen Fixation." The Nature Education Knowledge Project. 2011. nature.com/scitable/knowledge/library/biological-nitrogen-fixation -23570419/.

Walliser, Jessica. "Container Vegetable Plants: The Best Varieties for Success." Savvy Gardening (website). Accessed May 9, 2020. savvygardening.com/container-vegetable -plants-the-best-varieties/.

Woodard, Kathy. "Hanging Flower Baskets: 5 Secrets the Pros Use." The Garden Glove (website). Last updated April 2, 2020. thegardenglove.com/hanging-baskets-5-secrets -the-pros-use/.

Index

Page numbers in italics refer to photographs.

About the Authors

© Rob Normandeau

SHERYL NORMANDEAU was born and raised in the Peace Country region of northern Alberta and has made Calgary her home since 1994. A writer and master gardener, Sheryl holds a bachelor's degree in English, as well as a Prairie Horticulture Certificate and an Urban Sustainable Agriculture Certificate. Since 2013, she has served as the online Ask an Expert for the Calgary Horticultural Society. She works at the Calgary Public Library—besides gardening, books of all kinds are her grand passion! She is a small-space gardener (on a tiny balcony and in a plot in a nearby community garden) and she is most enthusiastic about growing veggies. She lives with her husband, Rob, and their rescue cat, Smudge. Find Sheryl at Flowery Prose (floweryprose .com) and on Facebook (@FloweryProse), Twitter (@Flowery_Prose), and Instagram (flowery_prose).

 **JANET MELROSE** was born in Trinidad, West Indies, and immigrated to Canada in 1964. She has lived in Calgary since 1969. She is a master gardener and the creator and owner of the successful horticulture business Calgary's Cottage Gardener, which specializes in garden education, horticultural therapy, and advocating for sustainable local food systems. She holds bachelor's degrees in sociology and history, a Prairie Horticulture Certificate, and a Horticultural Therapy Certificate. Janet is a lifelong gardener, coming from a heritage of English gardening. She has a large garden at home in the suburbs of Calgary that can only be described as a typical cottage garden. She cares for eight other gardens throughout Calgary through her work as a horticultural therapist, as well as a bed at the Inglewood Community Garden. She is married to Steve (for a long time), and they have two children, Jennifer and David. Three cats, Patrick, Theo, and Mia, currently own their home and patrol against the deer, hares, squirrels, skunk, mice, and assorted birds that believe the garden is theirs, too! Connect with Janet on Facebook (@calgaryscottagegardener), Twitter (@CalCottageGrdnr), and Instagram (CalgarysCottageGardener).

NOTES

NOTES

About the Series

It looks like you've discovered the **Guides for the Prairie Gardener.** This budding series puts the combined knowledge of two lifelong prairie gardeners at your grubby fingertips. Whether you've just cleared a few square feet for your first bed of veggies or are a seasoned green thumb stumped by that one cultivar you can't seem to master, we think you'll find Janet and Sheryl the ideal teachers. Find answers on seeds, soil, trees, flowers, weather, climate, pests, pots, and quite a few more. These slim but mighty volumes, handsomely designed, make great companions at the height of summer in the garden trenches and during cold winter days planning the next season. With regional expertise, elegance, and a sense of humour, Janet and Sheryl take your questions and turn them into prairie gardening inspiration. For more information, and for other titles in the series, visit touchwoodeditions.com/guidesprairiegardener.

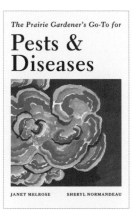